Ancient Peoples and Places

THE
ABYSSINIANS

General Editor

DR. GLYN DANIEL

ABOUT THE AUTHOR

Though the sciences were the subject of his formal studies at Trinity College, Cambridge University, it was as an M.A. (Cantab.) that David Buxton put the seal upon his academic training. In 1933, already a dedicated traveler, he left for tropical Africa as a professional entomologist. Nine years later, during World War II, he was sent from West Africa to Ethiopia. While there, he had ample opportunity to study various aspects of the country, especially the then little-known medieval churches. His firsthand investigations were resumed when he revisited Ethiopia in 1969. In 1949, Mr. Buxton published a book entitled Travels in Ethiopia *(reprinted in 1957), and he has, from time to time, contributed articles to journals both learned and popular. A fellow of the Society of Antiquaries, he is currently a research fellow of Clare Hall, Cambridge University.*

THE
ABYSSINIANS

David Buxton

128 PHOTOGRAPHS
45 LINE DRAWINGS
4 MAPS
2 TABLES

 PRAEGER PUBLISHERS
New York · Washington

THIS IS VOLUME SEVENTY-ONE IN THE SERIES

Ancient Peoples and Places

GENERAL EDITOR: DR. GLYN DANIEL

BOOKS THAT MATTER

Published in the United States of America in 1970
by Praeger Publishers Inc.
111 Fourth Avenue, New York, N.Y. 10003
© 1970 in London, England, by David Buxton
All rights reserved
Library of Congress Catalog Card Number: 79-112633
Printed in Great Britain

CONTENTS

5

ILLUSTRATIONS

Preface

FOLLOWING THE EXAMPLE of several other authors, I have applied the term 'Abyssinians' specifically to the Semitic-speaking peoples who still dominate the Ethiopian scene, and 'Abyssinia' to their historic mountain homeland which is, of course, only a part of modern Ethiopia. To non-English readers I would explain that these words have absolutely nothing opprobrious about them (on the contrary, they have romantic associations) and I trust no Ethiopians or others will object to their use.

Even though my subject matter is thus limited to the Abyssinians proper I have found it most difficult to cover the ground, however sketchily, in the space available. Indeed I am aware that there is little or no reference to certain important themes, for instance to land tenure and taxation, or to the theological position of the Ethiopian Church. The fact is that anyone attempting a general survey soon discovers the limits of his competence and is influenced willy-nilly by his personal tastes and interests. Therefore, such originality as the book possesses will be found mainly in the chapters on the arts, especially architecture, which became my favourite subject of study when I was living in Ethiopia between 1942 and 1949.

It would be difficult to list all the writings on Ethiopia which I have used and found profitable at one time or another and which have therefore influenced this book. The bibliography is limited to works which I actually consulted while compiling the text, many of them summary works. For this reason the great travellers of the nineteenth century, and most of the arm-chair *éthiopisants* of the last generation, are left unmentioned, though their work permeates the whole field of Ethiopian studies. I hope I am fully alive to the debt we owe to all these pioneers.

A word or two must be said about the spellings of Ethiopian words and place names. I feel that nothing would be gained, in a book of this kind, by adhering to any rigid system of transliteration. We have not enough vowels to equate to those occurring in the local languages, the great problem being how to represent the neutral vowel of the first form and the very short vowel—if it has one at all—of the sixth form (see Appendix A). Devotees of consistency must either use special phonetic symbols and diacritical marks—all unfamiliar and confusing to the non-specialist reader—or be content with some simpler system which is bound to lead to mispronunciation. I have simply adopted such spellings as give an idea how the words are spoken. However, since our alphabet has a useful spare symbol (q) I have followed many precedents in using it to represent the Ethiopian exploded 'K'.

One place name—admittedly an extreme case—will illustrate the difficulties of transliteration. An important village in Tigrai has been variously spelt: Agroo, Corou, Oucro, Ouqro, Ucro, Ouaqero, Oukero, Ouogro, Uogoro, Woghuro, Wogro, Waqro, and Weqro. Some of these forms, allowing for the fact that they are influenced by French or Italian spelling conventions, give a fair approximation to the name of the place as spoken, but the last two, while perfectly legitimate transliterations, have rather misleading first vowels. I have therefore preferred Wuqro.

This is not an expert treatise. But some fields of Ethiopian study have been explored—at least until very recently—by non-experts alone. Fortunately the old-fashioned scholar-adventurer may still find something exciting and unrecorded on his wanderings and can still contribute usefully to the study of the country. Hence, perhaps, Ethiopia's perennial fascination.

In conclusion I wish to record, with gratitude, that the generosity of Clare Hall, Cambridge, and the hospitality of the Faculty of Oriental Studies in this University, have greatly facilitated my recent work on Ethiopia, including the writing of this book.

D.R.B.

which occurred in the Tertiary Era when many other principal mountain ranges of the world were also being built up. Apparently the Ethiopian area was being gradually uplifted in the form of a dome whose centre would have coincided roughly with the central province of Shoa. At the same time there were extensive outpourings of very fluid lavas (chiefly basalts) and these flows—whose total thickness amounted in some areas to thousands of metres—were the material out of which the typical highland landscape was ultimately carved. Individual flows, too, could have notable side-effects: one lava dam produced Lake Tana; another cut off an arm of the sea and so caused the formation of the dry salt-lakes of northern Danakil.

While most of our area was subjected to upheaval, other long-continued stresses in the earth's crust led to the formation of the faulted trough known as the Rift Valley. This cuts right through the Ethiopian highlands and widens northwards to include the Danakil depression and the Red Sea. The Ethiopian Rift in the vicinity of Addis Ababa is ill-defined and no big escarpment is developed—a fact of which medieval invaders took advantage, as did those who built the railway from the coast in the present century. South of the capital the Rift becomes a well-marked geographical feature about 80 km. across which, with its attrac-tive lakes, contributes enormously to the interest and variety of the landscape.

The central and northern highlands of Ethiopia, the homeland of the Abyssinians proper, offer the traveller a succession of dramatic landscapes unparalleled in Africa. The plateau, usually cold and windswept, was no doubt originally a monoton-ous plain sloping gently towards the west and north-west. But the effect of erosion, during the millions of years that have elapsed since Tertiary times, has been to carve spectacular gorges, hundreds of metres deep, which open up abruptly in the gently undulating surface of the high plateau. Their walls may be precipitous throughout, or they may descend in steps so that

Plates 10–11

inhabited 'shelves' alternate with basaltic cliffs, and a deep gorge can provide a series of different climates. Similarly the plateau falls away with remarkable abruptness to the east—to the hot Danakil plains over 2,000 metres below. (This great escarpment forms part of the Rift Valley system though, owing to its greatly eroded state, the actual faults are mainly obscured.) In some areas denudation has progressed further and very little level country remains, except in the form of isolated inaccessible hilltops—the classic type of *amba* which, as fortress or prison, has played a notable part in Ethiopian history. Among the foot-hills of the Semien mountains there are many columns and pinnacles of rock of extraordinary form, some still retaining flat summits which are a vestige of the original plateau.

CLIMATE, SEASONS AND VEGETATION

Though Ethiopia lies within the tropics, only its outlying regions have a genuinely tropical climate. The highlands so characteristic of the country enjoy a climate which varies, according to altitude, from sub-tropical to temperate. However, the seasons typical of higher latitudes—depending as they do on wide variations in temperature through the year—are unknown here. Temperatures, though they differ enormously from place to place according to height above sea-level, vary only slightly in the course of the year. The factor which does vary, and which therefore controls the Ethiopian seasons, is the rainfall.

The Abyssinians have their own terms for three main climatic zones, which have been roughly defined as follows:

ZONE	HEIGHT	CLIMATE	AVERAGE TEMP.
Dega	above 2,400 m. (c. 8,000 ft)	temperate	16°C (61°F)
Woina dega	1,800–2,400 m. (c 6,000–8,000 ft)	sub-tropical	22°C (72°F)
Kwolla	below 1,800 m. (c. 6,000 ft)	tropical	26°C (c. 80°F) and over

So broken and complicated is Ethiopian highland topography that one may descend to *woina dega* (highland warm enough for the vine) and climb again to *dega* simply by crossing a valley, and every market is attended by inhabitants of two or even all three zones, bringing products appropriate to each.

The seasonal distribution of rainfall in the central and northern highlands resembles the monsoonal regime of the Indian sub-continent, the rainy months being those of the northern summer— late June to early September. Since the moisture-laden winds of the Ethiopian 'monsoon' blow from the south-west, it is the south-western highlands, where these winds first impinge on hill country, that have the most rain and the longest rainy season. Conversely, on reaching the far north these winds have already lost most of their water-vapour, and even the high upland regions—such as those of Eritrea—have too little rain, besides a shorter wet season than the country further south. On an average the rains cease about the time of the Ethiopian New Year in early September and there follows a long dry season lasting until February. Then lesser rains may occur in March, April or May, but these vary greatly from place to place and from season to season. The precipitation for the year in the central highlands probably averages about 1,000 mm. (37.4 in.).

The Danakil plains, lying as they do in the lee or the 'rain shadow' of the highlands, receive almost no rain during the highland wet season, though the floods of the Awash produce extensive seasonal grasslands. However, a little rain may fall in January and February when the highlands are dry. At that time of year winds blow inland from the Red Sea and masses of cloud may sometimes be seen banked against the eastern escarpment.

With its great range of altitude and hence of climate, Ethiopia possesses a wealth of vegetation types from sparse desert scrub to the most luxuriant forest. In parts of the south and south-west the ample rainfall (up to 2,000 mm.) and extended rainy season, together with sub-tropical temperatures, have favoured the growth of real rain-forests. They comprise a great variety of trees supporting a lush growth of climbers and epiphytes. This is the natural habitat of wild rubber, and of the native coffee bush which contributes so usefully, today, to Ethiopia's export trade.

In the central and northern highlands there is far too short a wet season for rain-forest and the cold would usually be an inhibiting factor, but types of dryer 'temperate' forest are known. Forests of *Podocarpus* occur below 2,200 m. (*c.* 7,000 ft) and of *Juniperus* ('Pencil Cedar') above that level, though the ranges of these two dominant species may overlap. Both have been sadly decimated by man. The wholesale destruction of the Pencil Cedar (locally called *tid*) around Addis Ababa almost caused the abandonment of that city about 1890, the situation being saved only by the introduction of fast-growing *Eucalyptus* from Australia. This tree now abounds in every inhabited place and has come to seem an essential ingredient in the highland landscape.

The real Abyssinians feel at home on the bleak and lofty plateau—the *dega*—some of which lies as high as 3,000 m. (10,000 ft) or more. The plateau is now for the most part devoid of forest whose former extent can only be judged from the splendid groves surrounding churches, where no trees may be cut. However, the occasional *tid* has been spared and likewise the occasional *kosso* (*Hagenia abyssinica*). This tree is not only an ornament to the landscape but provides the vermifuge indispensable to a people who are chronic sufferers from the tape-worm. The prevailing vegetation is a short grass cover forming a good walking surface and excellent grazing. Given some shelter, these lands will also yield cool-country crops like barley and beans. At still higher levels, up to and above 4,000 m., a remarkable 'Afro-Alpine' association occurs, including Giant Heath, Giant Lobelia and Everlastings. It corresponds to the weird vegetation of the high East African mountains, though the 'Tree Groundsel' (*Senecio*) has not yet been reported.

THE FLUX OF PEOPLES IN THE HORN OF AFRICA

There are traces in many parts of Ethiopia of Stone Age inhabitants from the later Palaeolithic onwards, and an important early Palaeolithic site (going right back to the 'Pebble Culture') is now being explored at Malka Qonturé in Shoa. Existing knowledge of these cultures is fragmentary, and depends largely on sporadic finds of stone implements. These data have been supplemented in recent years by the discovery of prehistoric rock-paintings and engravings which have been mainly confined, as yet, to two widely separated areas—Eritrea and Tigrai in the north, and the Harar region in the east. They have been described by P. Graziosi, who finds stylistic parallels to these paintings in the Neolithic rock-art of the Iberian peninsula and also in South Africa. Discussing the earlier Eritrean examples, he concludes that they were the work of a pastoral population which lived here before the arrival of humped cattle, and before the first appearance of Semitic-speaking immigrants from southern Arabia—both these events being dated to the first millennium B C.

It has not yet been possible to trace the connection between these prehistoric cultures and the peoples who came to occupy the Horn of Africa in later times. The essential fact, for our purposes, is that all this part of Africa was inhabited since the early dawn of history by people of Hamitic stock. Whatever their ultimate origin the Hamites became the exclusive possessors of most of north and east Africa before the advent of the Negroes, with whom, in east-central Africa, some of them later interbred.

The overwhelming majority of the Ethiopian population is still to be classed as Hamitic or predominantly Hamitic, and many sections still speak the 'Cushitic' languages proper to this family of peoples. The only major ethnic or cultural admixture we have to consider is that of the immigrant Semites from southern Arabia, who, whether by warlike or by peaceful means, imposed their language and their institutions on the Hamites of the northern highlands. The traditions they established and the

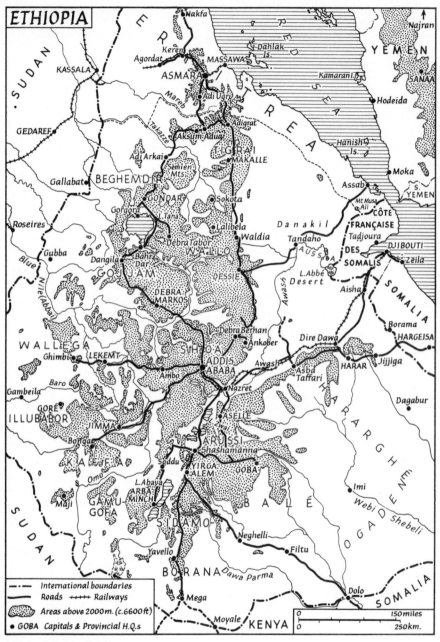

Fig. 1   Topographical map

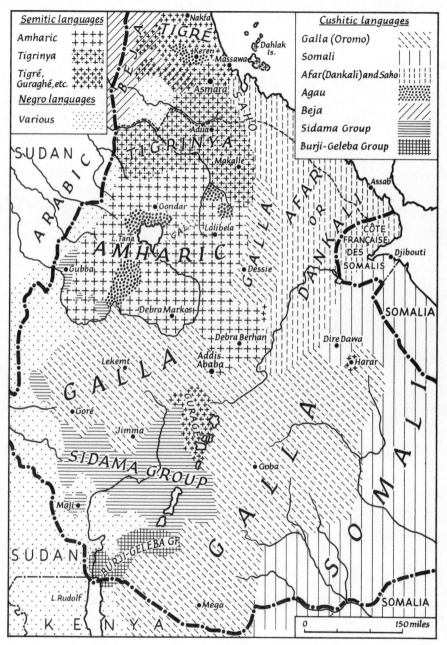

Semitic languages
Amharic +++
Tigrinya
Tigré, Guraghé, etc.
Negro languages
Various

Cushitic languages
Galla (Oromo)
Somali
Afar (Dankali) and Saho
Agau
Beja
Sidama Group
Burji-Geleba Group

Nakfa
TIGRÉ
Dahlak Is.
Keren
Massawa
Asmara
SUDAN
Adua
TIGRINYA
Makalle
Gondar
Lalibela
Assab
L.Tana
GALLA
CÔTE FRANÇAISE DES SOMALIS
Djibouti
AMHARIC
Dessie
Gubba
SOMALIA
Debra Markos
Debra Berhan
Dire Dawa
Lekemt
Addis-Ababa
Harar
GALLA
Goré
GURAGHÉ
Jimma
Goba
SIDAMA GROUP
GALLA
Maji
Goba
SUDAN
BURJI-GELEBA GP.
SOMALIA
L.Rudolf
Mega
SOMALIA
KENYA
0   150 miles

Fig. 2   Language map

culture they brought with them, as developed and expanded in Ethiopia, form the basic subject-matter of this book.

Figs. 1–2
The map showing languages and peoples should be perused in conjunction with the physical and provincial map on the opposite page. It presents the distribution of the principal peoples of Ethiopia at the present time, and it would be impossible to construct such a map for any earlier period in history. It must be remembered, however, that the distribution of these peoples during the many centuries surveyed in this volume was changing continuously, and the great immigration of the Gallas, which transformed the ethnic scene in this area, took place no longer ago than the fifteenth and sixteenth centuries A D.

If the upper halves of both maps are first inspected, it will be seen that the northern highlands are the home of those Hamites who absorbed a Semitic culture and still speak Semitic or 'semitized' languages. Long before the beginning of the Christian era a distinctively Ethiopian civilization had already emerged in this area, based on the royal and sacred city of Axum, later to become the holy place of Ethiopian Christianity.

Of the modern languages of this group the most northerly in distribution is Tigré (a name not to be confused with that of Tigré, or Tigrai, province further south). The speakers of this language are mostly nomad tribesmen inhabiting the lower hill country and the real lowlands of Eritrea, also some adjoining Sudan territory and the desolate Dahlak islands. The majority of them belong to the Beni Amer tribal complex—Hamites of rather pure blood who are said to be living replicas of the pre-dynastic Egyptians. (Other Beni Amer groups speak Beja, a Cushitic language, while some small sections are bilingual.) Nearly all Tigré-speakers are now Moslem, though some professed Monophysite Christianity even as late as the nineteenth century. It is interesting that this particular language of the Semitic family should now be associated neither with other aspects of Semitic culture, nor with Christianity.

The Tigreans and Amharas, speakers of the two principal Plates 1-8 Semitic languages of Ethiopia, are settled agriculturists of the plateau, living in the highland regions of Eritrea, Tigrai, Beghemdir, Wallo, Gojjam and Shoa. It is they who share the traditions of the Axum kingdom and we shall revert to them in this and later chapters. It must be pointed out now, however, that a number of pockets of non-semitized Hamites, remnants of the general population before the intrusion of Semitic influence, still exist on the plateau and still, to some extent, retain their own languages. These are the Agau groups shown on the map, the most northerly being the Bogos or Bilen in Eritrea, sandwiched between Tigrinya- and Tigré-speaking populations. Further south they occur round the northern shores of Lake Tana and in the district of Lasta, where an Agau dynasty—the Zagwé— ruled in the twelfth and thirteenth centuries. Another large group occupies part of that Amhara stronghold, the province of Gojjam (whence the district name of Agaumidir) and reaches south to the Blue Nile.

One of these residual communities has attracted particular atten- tion because of its very strong Hebraic and non-Christian tradi- tion. They are the Falasha, who live near Lake Tana (where some speak an Agau dialect) and extend thence northwards towards the Semien mountains. In Ullendorff's belief, expressed in *The Ethiopians*:

The Falashas are descendants of those elements in the Aksumite kingdom who resisted conversion to Christianity. In that case their so-called Judaism is merely the reflection of those Hebraic and Judaic practices and beliefs which were implanted on parts of south-west Arabia in the first post-Christian centuries and subsequently brought into Abyssinia. They are ignorant of Hebrew and their prayers and scriptures are written in Ghe'ez. Nevertheless the Falasha have in the past been regarded as the Jews—'Black Jews'—of Abyssinia, and they style themselves *beta Israel* or 'House of Israel'. They were viewed as a thorn in the flesh by Ethiopian emperors who frequently harried but never quite succeeded in subduing or converting them.

In *Ethiopia and the Bible* the same authority, again deprecating any tendency to exaggerate the Judaic character of this people, thus sums the matter up:

> Falashas and Ethiopians in general are the heirs of a civilization in which the veneration and imitation of the Old Testament occupy a central and enduring position.

The deeply entrenched and almost impassable valley of the Abbai or Blue Nile, where it forms the southern boundary of Gojjam, is one of the more clearly defined ethnic boundaries in Ethiopia. South of the river the population is solidly Galla, except to the west where Negroid tribes who have pushed in from the White Nile occupy most of the lower country. It has already been said that the Galla—another Hamitic people—were absent from Ethiopian territory in medieval times, though their ancestors must have been multiplying in what is now Somali country, south of the Gulf of Aden. These interesting people, with their highly developed tribal organization and characteristic institutions, outgrew their living space and started migrating in a south-westerly direction towards the end of the fifteenth century. In the sixteenth century, taking advantage of the universal chaos following the Moslem wars, the Gallas flooded into the southern marches of Ethiopia.

As a result of this wholesale immigration, and in spite of the ferocious resistance of various Ethiopian monarchs, the Galla came to occupy a great part of the plateau as far north as Wallega, Shoa and the region of Harar. They also occupied (with less difficulty) large tracts of the intermediate levels, as for instance the escarpment region of Wallo, where they form a 'buffer' community between the Amhara of the highlands and the Danakil of the desert. Some believe that the Galla have become, numerically, the largest single element in the population of Ethiopia. Of the principal non-semitized peoples, they have shown the greatest capacity for integration with the Amhara. The vast majority have abandoned the nomadic life. Many have adopted the Christian faith and, since Menelik's day, have risen to high positions in all walks of life, often as military commanders.

A further glance at the language map will show that some other peoples share south-western Ethiopia with the Galla. Alone among these the Guraghé speak a language of Semitic affinities whose origins are mysterious. The remainder are non-semitized Hamites speaking languages of the Cushitic family but not closely related to other Cushitic tongues: they are shown as the Sidama Group and the Burji-Geleba Group. The discontinuous distribution of those two language groups suggests that the tribes employing them were very much more widespread before the invasions of the Gallas, who are known to have displaced them from wide areas. Still further to the south-west the border country is inhabited by little-known Negroid tribes whose territory extends to the White Nile and its tributaries.

Fig. 2

It remains to say something of the nomad tribes of the eastern plains. The Somali who now range over the 'Horn' of Africa in the narrower sense must have arrived there in comparatively recent times: part of their country was that vacated by the Galla only a few hundred years ago. Somali country includes not only the large new state of Somalia but much of north-eastern Kenya and the Ethiopian Ogaden; while in French Somaliland they meet the Danakil at the northern extremity of their range. It is an enormous area of more or less arid country, thinly peopled by nomadic groups whose livelihood and mode of living depend almost entirely on the camel.

Further north the Danakil (or Afar), together with their kin, the Saho, occupy a large triangle of desert based on the Red Sea, limited to the west by the great wall of the escarpment and to the

south by the highlands which extend to Harar. Though season,
ally mitigated by the flood water of the Awash, conditions here,
especially in northern Danakil, are the hottest and most in,
hospitable to be found in Ethiopia. The Danakil nomads,
notorious for their ferocity when raiding—strange in a people who
feed on little else but milk—live in small domed huts made of
grass matting, which are easily loaded on to camel,back when
they move on to the next pasturage.

Though Hamites, these wandering peoples, who share the
slight, long,limbed build of the nomad, have little in common
with the settled population of the highlands. Yet it would be a
mistake to suppose that they have played no part in Ethiopian
history. On the contrary, warlike by nature and Moslem in faith,
these were the very people who, under forceful command, were
ever ready and anxious to attack the Christians of the plateau.
This they were doing intermittently for hundreds of years, until
the highland kingdom was brought to the verge of extinction in
the sixteenth century.

THE SEMITIC INHERITANCE

The south,Arabian immigrants already referred to brought a
Semitic culture to Africa including at least one south,Arabian
dialect. However, the cutting,off of this new Semitic territory
from its Arabian roots, and the considerable influence of the
indigenous Cushitic tongues, soon resulted in the evolution of a
new local language. This, the official language of the Axumite
Appendix A   kingdom, is known locally as Ghe'ez, and in the West as
Ethiopic. Though apparently short,lived as a spoken language
it was of cardinal importance in the development of Abyssinian
civilization. It became, like Latin in the West, the classical
language of literature and of the Church and as such has con,
tinued in use ever since. Furthermore, Ghe'ez was the ancestor
of the modern languages whose descent has been elucidated by
Ullendorff in these words:

In order to convey an idea of the relationship of Amharic, Tigrinya and Tigré towards each other and towards Ghe'ez, we might enlist the helpful parallel of the Romance languages. If Ghe'ez is compared to Latin, Tigrinya takes the place of Italian (both because it is most closely akin to the 'parent'/ tongue and also on account of its continuance in the original home). Tigré would then be likened to Spanish and Amharic to French (also because it has been subjected to the most far/ reaching changes).

The principal influence which served to differentiate these languages, just as it had helped to differentiate Ghe'ez, was that of the native Cushitic tongues, especially Agau. These were then spoken, of course, by the mass of the population, though they survive only in small enclaves today.

Just as their language is nearest to the ancient tongue, so the Tigreans themselves must be regarded as the direct inheritors of the Axumite kingdom in whose territory they still live. The Amharas were to carry the tradition further afield to the south/ west and south. It was they who became eventually the dominant, as well as the most numerous, of these two kindred populations, and their language is now becoming the *lingua franca* of the whole country. Amharas and Tigreans together constitute the Abyssini/ ans proper, a term which serves to distinguish them from the many other peoples inhabiting modern Ethiopia, all of whom, whatever their history and traditions, are Ethiopians. This book is concerned with the Abyssinians as so defined, and especially with the unique Christian culture which developed in their kingdom from the fourth century onwards.

Those who have studied the Abyssinians or lived among them know how completely their society differs from that of the old pagan, tribal, Africa. In fact it has been said with some justice that Abyssinia is in Africa, but not of it. Also, it may be said that it exists in the present but belongs rather to the past. Ever since

Westerners began to travel there they have felt transported, on their journeys, to other times and places—usually to biblical lands and to Old Testament times.

Such a sensation is not entirely subjective. The Abyssinians do regard themselves as the true successors of Israel, believe their royal house to be descended from Solomon, and use *tabots* in their Christian worship which represent the Ark of the Covenant. They revere the Old Testament as much as the New and have incorporated, in their social system, many Mosaic precepts drawn from the Books of Leviticus and Deuteronomy. (Examples are the dietary prohibitions, especially of pork; the practice of circumcision on the eighth day; the conception of ritual uncleanness which bars people from church after sexual intercourse, etc.; the practice of marrying a brother's widow; the prescribed method of administering a flogging.)

The Church, too, shows apparently Jewish influence, especially in the observance of the double Sabbath (Saturday as well as Sunday). And there is the liturgical dance of the Abyssinians, performed by *dabtaras* in the presence of the *tabot* (as it might have been performed by levites in the presence of the ark) with beating of drums and sistra and prayer-sticks. This scene has reminded generations of travellers of the passage in II Samuel 6, when David and the house of Israel played before the Lord with all manner of instruments, and danced before the Lord with all their might, and brought up the ark of the Lord with shouting.

Plate 12

There is no doubt, therefore, of the far-reaching influence of the Old Testament on various aspects of Abyssinian life, and no doubt that a biblical atmosphere can really be breathed there. In spite of this, I have myself always been more conscious of the *medieval* character of the Abyssinian rural scene, for the old provinces of Ethiopia were until very recently a real feudal country and the quasi-feudal hierarchy, as well as the hierarchy of the Church, still enjoy their old prestige.

Travelling in Abyssinia in close touch with the people is an experience which constantly calls up one's mental picture of early medieval Europe. The stone-built huts of the northern Plates 15-18 provinces, with their slit-like windows high in the walls, have open hearths so that smoke blackens the roof-timbers and finds its way out through the thatch. The domestic compound with its high surrounding wall and even (sometimes) a defensive gatehouse harbours the farmer's stock at night and is well barricaded against animal or human intruders. Trade is mainly by barter in the great markets and all goods are transported by pack-animals. Dignitaries move about the countryside in stately fashion on muleback, clustered around with attendants on foot. Wandering minstrels attend at festivals and celebrations.

As in the Middle Ages, again, Mother Church permeates the whole of life; priests are indispensable members of the community and enjoy enormous respect. So do the monks, and Abyssinian monasteries have always been the guardians, not only of Christian doctrine, but of art and literature. Famed sanctuaries up and down the country are the resort of pilgrims from far and near, and the holy manuscripts slung from their shoulders are still written out on parchment by the monastic scribes. Plate 6

Whichever way the traveller's mind is oriented, his experience in this antique land cannot fail to be abundantly rewarding. Nor will those whose main interest is in the present be disappointed, for this unusual and attractive people, with their remarkable history behind them, are still capable of great things. Ethiopia has now joined the main stream of contemporary events, and is bound to play a great part in African and world affairs in the future.

CHAPTER II

The Abyssinians : their History

THE EARLIEST CIVILIZATION

THE FIRST BOOK OF KINGS and the Second Book of Chronicles both describe how the Queen of Sheba, lured by Solomon's fame, journeyed to Jerusalem with a great train and costly presents and there 'communed with him of all that was in her heart'. King Solomon for his part 'gave to the Queen of Sheba all her desire. . . . So she turned, and went to her own land, she and her servants'. Again, St Matthew's Gospel recalls how the Queen of the South 'came from the ends of the earth to hear the wisdom of Solomon'. These events supposedly occurred about 970 BC.

In Ethiopia itself she is known as either the Queen of Sheba or (as in the New Testament) the Queen of the South, and she is also given a local name, Makeda. The *Kebra Nagast* or 'Book of the Glory of Kings' of the Abyssinians provides a detailed account of how the Queen was seduced by Solomon to whom, after her return home, she bore a son. When this prince had grown up he travelled to Jerusalem himself and eventually came back to his own country bringing with him the Ark of the Covenant which he and his companions had stolen from the Temple. He was Menelik I, the founder of the Abyssinian royal house.

This legend, belief in which is an article of faith among the Abyssinians, may possibly contain some germ of historical fact. The same legend (with minor variations) is known among the peoples of southern Arabia who contributed the important Semitic element in the Abyssinians' heritage. Indeed Sheba or Saba was the name of a kingdom in what is now the Yemen from which these ancestral Abyssinians later emigrated. Their queen, Bilqis to the Arabs, could quite possibly have travelled to Jerusalem in Old Testament times.

Abyssinian history proper begins with the migration of these south-Arabian tribes to the western side of the Red Sea during the first millennium B C. The immigrants were not nomads but a settled agricultural population seeking an extension of their living-space. They colonized what we should now call the northern extremity of the Ethiopian plateau. One important group was the Ghe'ez who settled in the southern Eritrean highlands which are most accessible from the sea and whose particular dialect was eventually adopted by most of the inhabitants. An-other tribe were the Habashat who settled further south, in Tigrai, and whose name (of which 'Abyssinia' is a corruption) came to be applied to the whole people and country. Here they apparently formed a ruling caste among the indigenous Hamites, who are still represented today by various Agau groups.

In what sense these immigrants were the founders of the old Abyssinian kingdom is a matter of dispute. Their impact probably took the form of gradual infiltration rather than armed conquest. In any case, there is ample evidence of the enormous political and cultural influence they exerted in their new home. As stated earlier, their modified south-Arabian language, which re-tained the name of Ghe'ez, always continued in use for literary and liturgical purposes while the modern languages developed from it. The syllabary in which it was written (Sabean or Himyaritic), though later forgotten in the land of its birth, became the alphabet in which the Abyssinian languages are written—and printed—today. Moreover the early kingdom was dominated, until the advent of Christianity, by the cult of the old south-Arabian gods.

Appendix A
Plates 25-30

No doubt there is much else in the Abyssinians' mode of life—especially in their agriculture, which remains the basis of their economy—that could be traced back to those Arabian highlands from which the Semitic immigrants had sprung. The laboriously terraced slopes and gullies of the Yemen mountains, with their complicated systems of irrigation, are closely paralleled among the gorges and escarpments of the Abyssinian plateau. And one can hardly doubt that the plough—unknown in 'black' Africa—was one more invaluable gift to Abyssinia on the part of these early settlers.

The attractive village of Yeha (formerly Ava) lying to the north of the Adua–Adigrat road seems to have been the headquarters or at least a principal city of the pre-Axumite kingdom. Its diminutive acropolis is crowned by a church (modern, but of early foundation) and by the far more ancient temple-ruins described elsewhere (p. 86). Though no other architecture of the period can be compared with these impressive remains, recent excavations at Yeha and at other pre-Axumite sites have brought to light important statuary, a splendid throne, and other objects of religious significance. There are also stone slabs, altars and censers bearing inscriptions which at this early period (fifth to fourth century BC) are 'boustrophedon', i.e. the lines run alternately from right to left and left to right, the letters (where not symmetrical) pointing in the appropriate direction. In these inscriptions the name of 'LMQH, the moon-god, nearly always appears (the south-Arabian syllabary showed no distinction between vowels so the name can be vocalized, according to taste, as Almaqah, Ilmuquh, etc.). Besides the crescent and disk which symbolize this divinity, his other attributes—the bull and the ibex—recur in the form of reliefs and statuettes.

Objects of everyday use, recovered in recent years by excavation, tell a good deal about this early Abyssinian civilization which flourished before the rise of Axum. They include some finely made pottery of very varied forms, several lamps and a variety of bronze tools and weapons including spears, daggers, axes, chisels and sickles. There are also the curious 'identity marks' which seem to have served as personal seals or monograms: their impressions have been found on pottery and they could have been used as brands for marking stock. No two are alike and they consist of open-work geometrical or animal designs often incorporating

Fig. 11

Plates 19–26

Fig. 3

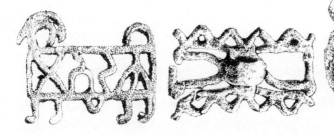

Fig. 3 'Identity marks' from pre-Axumite sites. These are unusually large examples measuring 8–11 cm.

a few characters of the alphabet—presumably abbreviations of the owner's name.

These finds have revealed a comparatively advanced culture which, though strongly influenced by southern Arabia, is yet different from anything known to have existed there. The Abyssinians already showed their special genius for absorbing but at the same time transmuting any novel ideas that came in from abroad.

THE AXUM KINGDOM AND THE COMING OF CHRISTIANITY

Though nothing is known of the circumstances, the pre-Axumite state began to decline in the third century B C. About the beginning of the Christian era a new power, based on different cities and almost wholly independent of south-Arabian influence, began to dominate the scene. Chief among the new cities was Axum which became the seat of the Abyssinian kings and the fountain-head of a new civilization. Modern Ethiopia is directly descended from the Axum kingdom. Even when, after a thousand years, the seat of government moved elsewhere, Axum, which by then had powerful Christian associations, remained for all time a holy place to the Abyssinians.

This kingdom, destined ultimately to an extreme degree of isolation, was a well-known power of classical times. Its link with the outer world was the port of Adulis on the Gulf of Zula, a sheltered inlet of the Red Sea south of Massawa. From Axum it took eight days to reach the port: one travelled via the lesser cities of the high plateau, Matara, Tokonda or Kohaito, after which came a tremendous descent of some 2,500 m. (8,000 ft) before traversing the arid plains to the Red Sea itself. Following in the wake of Ptolomaic expeditions which had explored these coasts in search of elephants, Greek mariners founded the port, which was certainly in use by the first century B C. Later (first century A D) the place and its trade was described in the *Periplus of the Erythraean Sea*—a work which also contains the first known literary reference to Axum.

Plate 36

Through this port, though its architecture remained purely Axumite, a whiff of Greek culture reached Axum, and a number of Greek inscriptions are known. Many early Axumite coins also have legends in Greek characters and the coins as a whole are similar in design to those of the Graeco-Roman world and evidently inspired by them. In exchange for the ivory exported through Adulis, foreign wares, including amphorae and glass vessels from the Mediterranean, were carried up to the Axumite cities. Through Adulis, Axum had trading links, if sporadic, with other distant countries, including Persia and India.

The military exploits of the kings of Axum were recorded in inscriptions which reveal them as great empire-builders. A

Fig. 4

notable monarch of the third century A D, Aphilas, not only enlarged his own kingdom but crossed the Red Sea and conquered parts of south-western Arabia which had been the homeland of his Semitic ancestors. The Greek inscription at Adulis which recorded these events was transcribed by Cosmas Indicopleustes, an Alexandrian merchant, in his *Christian Cosmography* (early sixth century A D)—a work which describes the coasts and cities of the Red Sea and Indian Ocean.

A great king of the fourth century, Ezana, left a number of inscriptions of which the first had parallel texts in three languages,

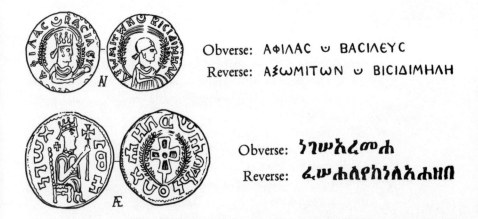

Obverse: ΑΦΙΛΑC ᴗ ΒΑCΙΛΕΥC

Reverse: ΑƺѠΜΙΤѠΝ ᴗ ΒΙϹΙΔΙΜΗΛΗ

Obverse: ነገሡእረመሐ

Reverse: ፈሡሐለየከነለእሐዘበ

Fig. 4 Axumite coins, slightly enlarged (after Littmann). Top, gold coin of Aphilas (third century) with pagan crescent-and-disk symbol and Greek inscription; below, bronze coin of Armah (seventh century) with cross and unvocalized Ghe'ez inscription. Reverse reads: 'Joy be to the peoples'

Greek, south Arabian and Ghe'ez. But his later inscriptions are in Ghe'ez only, which shows how its prestige was increasing, rendering the use of foreign languages superfluous. Ezana still claimed sovereignty over parts of south-western Arabia, but his recorded campaigns were directed against insurgent peoples within, or bordering upon, his own kingdom. His latest inscription records his conquest of the Nubian kingdom of Meroë on the Upper Nile whose great days coincided with those of Axum, though these neighbouring kingdoms had almost nothing in common and their contacts were apparently scanty.

Plate 27

The same inscription is of very exceptional interest in that Ezana attributes his success in battle not, as hitherto, to his household god, the 'unconquered Mahrem', but to the 'Lord of Heaven' and 'Lord of the Earth'. This important change in the tenor of a royal inscription indicated, albeit ambiguously, the king's conversion to the Christian faith. It may be that Ezana, in his prudence, thought the time not yet ripe for publicizing his recent change of faith throughout the kingdom, where the old gods were still honoured. But Ezana's conversion is attested (as Littmann first pointed out) by the coins of his reign: the earlier ones bear the crescent and disk, the later ones the cross—they were in fact among the earliest coins of any country to carry this Christian symbol.

The manner of the conversion is told by Rufinus, a near-contemporary Roman historian, and there is every reason to believe that his story is true in its essentials. One Meropius, a Christian philosopher of Tyre, went voyaging to improve his mind, 'taking with him two small boys who were related to him and whom he was educating in humane studies'. When, on the return voyage, the ship put in at some Red Sea port, Meropius and the whole ship's company were massacred by the coastal tribesmen. The account continues:

> The boys were found studying under a tree and preparing their lessons, and, preserved by the mercy of the Barbarians, were taken to the King. He made one of them, Aedesius, his cup-bearer. Frumentius, whom he had perceived to be sagacious and prudent, he made his treasurer and secretary. Thereafter they were held in great honour and affection by the King.

Frumentius gradually rose to a position of great influence and when the king, Ella Amida, died prematurely, leaving an infant son (who was Ezana) he was asked to assume the functions of Regent. At the same time he did all in his power to encourage the spread of the Christian religion, which was not unknown among foreign traders already resident in the country. When the young Ezana was of age to take over the government the two brothers left the kingdom, Aedesius returning home to Syria where Rufinus heard the whole extraordinary story from his own lips.

Frumentius, however, made for Alexandria so as to inform the Patriarchate of the Christian flock awaiting a shepherd in the distant kingdom of Axum. Athanasius, lately appointed Patriarch, chose Frumentius himself—though he cannot yet have been a priest—to return as bishop to his adopted country. There he continued his missionary endeavours which were rewarded eventually by the conversion of the king himself. The Abyssinians call their apostle Abba Salama (father of peace). The name of their first Christian ruler, Ezana, has dropped out of the popular memory, being replaced by those of the legendary twin kings, Abreha and Atsbeha; but there is no serious conflict between history and legend.

The consecration of Frumentius by the Patriarch of Alexandria resulted naturally in the Ethiopian Church becoming a dependency of the Monophysite Church of Egypt, a relationship not finally broken until 1958. (In theory, therefore, the Ethiopians accept the findings of the earlier ecumenical Councils of Nicaea, Constantinople and Ephesus, and the arch-heretics, Arius and Nestorius, are sometimes unflatteringly depicted in their churches. But, along with the Armenians, they reject the rulings of the Council of Chalcedon (AD 451) to which both the Western and the Eastern Orthodox Churches subscribe.)

The impressive material achievements of the Axumites, especially in architecture and the raising of the great monoliths, are described in a later chapter (IV). The third and fourth centuries seem to have been their most prosperous and most productive period, especially just before the conversion (c. AD 340); the modest beginnings of a new Christian architecture are not seen until two centuries later. No doubt there was literary activity as well (though nothing survives except inscriptions on stone), for the old south-Arabian syllabary had been reformed and greatly improved by the middle of the fourth century, probably under Ezana. That is to say, a system of vocalization was introduced, whereby each basic character could be modified in six ways according to the vowel sound it incorporates (see Appendix A). This was a most important step forward, and the

Plates 31–46

41

alphabet so modified has stood the test of time, for it is still in use, with some additions, today.

An outstanding event in Abyssinia's Christian history was the arrival, towards the end of the fifth century, of the 'Nine Saints'. They are thought to have been learned Syrian monophysites expelled from their native land after the Council of Chalcedon and seeking refuge in a country whose religious beliefs did not conflict with their own. It was they who brought monasticism (following the rule of St Pachomius) to Abyssinia, and they were probably the first to translate the Greek Scriptures into Ghe'ez. They loom large in local hagiography and some of their names are associated with specific monasteries. Thus Abuna Za-Mikael Aragawi was the founder of Debra Damo, which inaccessible mountain he is said to have first ascended with the aid of a monster serpent.

The Axumites were now firm Christians. The sixth-century kings, Kaleb and his son Gabra Masqal, have gone down in history as outstanding champions of the faith and the remains of their supposed tomb-chapels are to be seen on a hill-top near Axum. The Abyssinians' Arabian dominions were lost and, with them, their command of the sea. Then news reached the court that Dhu Nawas, a judaized king of Himyar, had started viciously persecuting the Christians of Nadjran (now in Saudi Arabia). Moved by the sufferings of his fellow-Christians, whose plight is recorded in Abyssinian poetry of a later age (p. 130), Kaleb, in AD 524, launched a campaign to succour them, a Greek fleet helping to transport his forces across the Red Sea. The campaign was successful. It led to the temporary re-establishment of Abyssinian rule in the Yemen (where a number of churches were built), and even to an attempted raid on Mecca, involving elephants, which is mentioned in the Koran. However, after the Persian conquest of Arabia, followed almost at once by the rise of Muhammad, the Axumites gave up any attempt to retain their footing there.

Early in the seventh century a king of Axum, Armah (well
known for his coins, which are very common) gave sanctuary to   *Fig. 4*
some of the first followers of Muhammad who had been driven
from Mecca, then still a pagan sanctuary. This gesture of tolerance
and hospitality for a time exempted Abyssinia from the *jihad*, the
'holy war' to which all those who resisted Islam were subject.
On the other hand the Arabs were sometimes provoked by the
depredations of supposedly Abyssinian pirates in the Red Sea,
who even sacked Jidda. In the end the Muhammadans, and
especially the nomads of the coastal plains on the African side,
who were early converts, became a perennial menace to the
Abyssinians' Christian kingdom. These early conquests on the
part of Islam were the beginning of that process of encirclement
which, with the destruction of Adulis, was to seal off Abyssinia
from the outer world. As Gibbon aptly expressed it:

Encompassed on all sides by the enemies of their religion, the
Aethiopians slept near a thousand years, forgetful of the world
by whom they were forgotten.

The declining years of the Axum kingdom share something
of the obscurity prevailing in contemporary Europe, when the
Carolingian Empire was breaking up and King Alfred was
fighting the Danes in southern England. The fortunes of the
kingdom fluctuated. For a brief period it was able to re-assert its
authority over the Red Sea coasts and even to extend it to the
Dahlak Islands and the distant port of Zeila on the Gulf of Aden.
But these were the flickerings of a candle about to be extinguished.
The kingdom, finally deprived of its outlet to the sea, stagnated
culturally and was troubled and weakened by the inroads of the
nomadic *Beja* (who still live in Eritrea) from the north. Most
significant of all, the native Agau people in the west and south
were in revolt against Axumite authority.

43

AGAU RULE AND THE EXCAVATION OF CHURCHES

Late in the tenth century A D a formidable Agau chieftainess called Gudit (or Judith) brought the thousand-year history of the Axum kingdom to a close. She overthrew their last king, killed the royal princes (confined at Debra Damo) and tried to uproot the Christian religion. In Abyssinian folklore this half-legendary figure is remembered as the great destroyer of churches, rivalled only by Ahmad Grañ six hundred years later.

This violent break with the Christian tradition proved only transitory. Gudit's more important contribution to history was the abandonment of Axum and the transfer of the seat of power to the Agau country much farther south. On a long view this can be seen as a necessary step in the integration of Abyssinia, for the native Agau people, hitherto subject to a Semitic or Semitized aristocracy, now gained the upper hand and distinctions of descent or class between rulers and ruled began to disappear.

The Agau monarchs who followed Gudit established their headquarters at Roha in Lasta, later renamed Lalibela after the most renowned of these kings, and they ruled for some three hundred years. They are known as the Zagwé dynasty (though the term should properly be restricted to the later members of the line, after 1137). They controlled an area more extensive than the Axum kingdom, most of it chaotically mountainous and traversed only by a limited number of difficult routes. It probably embraced the highlands of modern Eritrea and the whole of Tigrai, extending southwards to Waag, Lasta and Damot (Wallo province) and thence westwards towards Lake Tana (Beghemdir).

The Zagwés reverted passionately to the Christian religion and made great efforts to maintain the obligatory link with the Patriarchate of Alexandria. So great, however, were the difficulties of travel since the Arab conquests that for long periods Abyssinia remained without an Abuna (see page 74). Moreover the Moslem rulers of Egypt had to be bribed with expensive presents to cooperate in negotiations for a new Abuna, for they were jealous and suspicious of the Patriarch's links with the distant Christian kingdoms beyond Egypt's southern borders. However, the Egyptians' belief that the kings of Abyssinia had the power to divert the floodwaters of the Blue Nile—the life-blood of their own country—may have helped towards better relationships. (Threats to divert the Nile were used again by later Abyssinian kings—a fact known to Ariosto who refers to it in the thirty-third canto of *Orlando Furioso*.)

The link with Egypt was maintained in another way, for the Christian Copts were sometimes compelled by persecution to flee to other countries. Under Al-Hakim, before and after the year 1000, many of them reached Abyssinia, and it is likely that the artistic links with Coptic Egypt (mentioned in chapters VI and VII) resulted from this immigration. The centuries-old connection with Jerusalem also dates from the time of the Zagwés for in AD 1189 Saladin allotted the Chapel of the Invention of the Cross, in the Church of the Holy Sepulchre, to the Abyssinians. Their pilgrimage to Jerusalem and their monastic outpost there (though subsequently restricted to the roof of the chapel) has constituted an important link with the East-Christian world and a source of inspiration in art.

For this fascinating period of Abyssinian history there are no contemporary records. The king lists and chronicles that do exist were compiled retrospectively two or three hundred years later: they are full of contradictions and inconsistencies and are very largely legendary. One of these kings is remembered for his unexampled wisdom and piety and for the many miraculous events of his life. This was Lalibela (*c.* 1150–1220) to whom also the chronicle, and the local tradition, attributes the famous rock-hewn churches in the town that bears his name.

Plates 56–8

The hewing-out of the rock-churches, which abound in Tigrai as in Lasta, was an achievement almost unparalleled in history. It shows that the Zagwés attained a degree of stability and technical advancement seldom equalled in Abyssinian history; yet all objective record of these vast undertakings is lost. It is remarkable, too, that this land-locked kingdom should have maintained, in spite of all obstacles, some tenuous links with the main body of Christendom, and that it kept its Christian culture intact. The dynasty served Abyssinia well. Subsequent genera, tions acknowledged this, for though the Zagwé were regarded— owing to their non-Solomonic ancestry—as an illegitimate dynasty, Lalibela has always been revered as one of the great national saints.

THE RESTORED SOLOMONIC DYNASTY IN CONFLICT WITH THE RISING POWER OF ISLAM

It is recorded in the chronicles that the only Axumite prince not massacred by Gudit—his name was Dilna'ad—escaped to Shoa in the far south. About the year 1268 Yikuno Amlak, a chieftain of the Dessie region of Wallo, became king in succession to Nakueto La'ab, last of the Zagwés. He was able to claim descent from Dilna'ad, which ensured popular support for his cause and enabled him to defeat the Zagwé king in battle. However, according to a much later version of the story, Yikuno Amlak's accession was due to the diplomatic skill of the famous saint and statesman Tekla Haymanot who persuaded Nakueto La'ab to abdicate of his own free will so that the ancient line of Solomon could be restored. In recognition of Tekla Haymanot's services the king agreed (it is said) to hand over one-third of all the lands in the kingdom for the support of the Church.

The restored dynasty maintained their connection with Shoa, which meant that the political centre of gravity of the kingdom— now essentially an Amhara kingdom—moved once again southwards. The kings of the fourteenth and fifteenth centuries used Debra Berhan and other places in that area as their head, quarters—for the first, but by no means the last time in Ethiopian history. However, the times were constantly disturbed, and each king kept moving from one royal camp to another as he roamed the country to bring dissident provinces under control or repel attacks from outside. Comparative stability existed only in the great monastic centres which, as in medieval Europe, were the permanent guardians of the country's cultural heritage.

During these two centuries the excavation of rock-churches must have continued, though its main impulse had vanished with the passing of the Zagwés. Mural painting probably flourished, but too little remains of it to permit any real appreciation of its quality. On the other hand this was the period of a great literary revival and a certain number of original works appeared both in verse and prose. Scriptural books, including the Gospels, were copied out in large numbers and the arts both of calligraphy and illumination were eagerly cultivated (see chapters V and VI).

Amda Tsion I was the dominating figure of the first half of the fourteenth century. His immoralities as a young king earned him public reproofs from the monks of Debra Libanos, but he became a strong and statesmanlike ruler. His reign is chiefly remembered for the earliest serious conflicts with the gradually encroaching Moslem states, especially with Ifat which included all eastern Shoa and extended to the Red Sea coast. The final success of these campaigns was largely due to the king's extraordinary personal courage, celebrated in some martial songs which have survived. As a result, the danger of Ethiopia being absorbed into the Islamic world was for a time averted. There was even expansion at the Moslems' expense, but Harar remained the great bastion of their power.

Throughout the middle years of the fifteenth century Zar'a Yaqob, the self-styled Constantine of Abyssinia, kept the country under firm control. With single-minded brutality he persecuted the pagans as well as any Christians who were influenced by pagan beliefs or practices. Never hesitating to intervene in Church affairs he introduced many new annual and monthly festivals, revived the observance of Saturday as a second 'Sabbath', instructed his Christian subjects to wear crosses and had new religious books translated into Ghe'ez. He was himself the author of several books expounding his conception of Christian discipline, which was harsh in the extreme. In accordance with his policy of strengthening the south against the historic north he transferred the office and dignity of the *etcheghé* (head of the monasteries) from St Stephen's on Lake Hayq to the abbott of Debra Libanos in Shoa. (Apparently the king was not directly concerned with the Ethiopian delegation to the Council of Ferrara/Florence in 1440–41: this was sent on the authority of the prior of the Abyssinian monastery in Jerusalem.)

Like all kings of this period Zar'a Yaqob had to repel in-cursions from various Moslem states to the east and south. For centuries these had occupied the inhospitable plains between the highlands and the coast, but now they embraced most of southern Shoa and those neighbouring regions of the middle levels, Arussi and Bale. These states were a perennial menace and their forces made a habit of attacking during the months of the long Lenten fast when the Christians were weakened by abstinence. Nevertheless this king's reign saw the steady enlargement of the kingdom at the expense of both Moslem and pagan areas in the south and south-west.

Zar'a Yaqob's career illustrates the extraordinary difficulties which were the lot of many Abyssinian kings and explains a chronic weakness in the succession. It was the custom to keep all royal princes who might be pretenders to the throne in the forced seclusion of some well-guarded *amba* or flat-topped mountain, from which a new ruler would be fetched when required. Zar'a Yaqob was one of those who grew up in such a royal prison, deprived of all contact with ordinary people or ordinary life. Coming to the throne in 1434, with no experience of the affairs of state, he was faced by a kingdom seething with plots and rebel-lions, a Church riven with heresies, and outside enemies constantly threatening invasion. In the circumstances it was hardly possible for the new king to show adaptability or tolerance or diplomatic skill, which are the fruit of long experience in human relationships. Confronted with a desperate and chaotic situation he met it instead with grim determination and implacable ferocity. Towards the end of his life, forfeiting the affection and loyalty even of his courtiers and family he became a lonely figure, isolated by suspicion and mistrust. But, in spite of all, the name of this great defender of the faith is one of the most memorable in all Ethiopian history.

The Islamic states, especially Adal which had now absorbed Ifat, became more threatening during the fifteenth century. Sometimes they raided deep into the fertile and salubrious high-lands which were almost wholly in Christian hands and which the people of the plains not unnaturally coveted. Every emperor had to keep them at bay, though attempts were also made, about the end of the century, to reach a settlement by negotiation. Such peaceful overtures were at first encouraged by the Empress Helena, herself the daughter of a Moslem border-chieftain in southern Shoa. She had been one of the queens of Ba'eda Maryam (1467-78) and had lived on, gradually increasing her influence, through the two subsequent reigns.

Early in the sixteenth century it was the same aged empress, Helena, then acting as regent for the young king Lebna Denghel, who finally gave up the attempt to maintain peace with the Moslems. She asked Portugal for help against them, the Portu-guese being the only Europeans then to be found on the Red Sea coasts, which they were hotly disputing with the Turks. The Portuguese were, in fact, already interested in Abyssinia. Ever since the fourteenth century they had identified the legendary Prester John with the Abyssinian emperor and thought of him as a potential Christian ally in the east: this, at last, was an oppor-tunity to make contact with him. After years of delay, an embassy was dispatched from Goa in 1520 and it remained in the country

until 1526. The first meeting with 'Prester John' proved something of an anticlimax, but the experiences and adventures of the
mission, as recorded by their chaplain Francisco Alvares, make
fascinating reading.

In 1528 the great storm which had been gathering for centuries
broke over Abyssinia. The Imam Ahmad ibn Ibrahim alGhazi,
remembered in Abyssinia as Grañ (the 'lefthanded'), launched an
invasion from the region of Harar which was almost to obliterate
Abyssinia as a Christian state. This gifted fanatic had welded the
nomads, especially the Somalis of the eastern plains, into a
formidable fighting force, fired with the spirit of the *jihad*. They
left a trail of slaughter and pillage throughout the length and
breadth of the Christian highlands. The king became a fugitive
hunted from one mountain retreat to another and died prematurelyly. The destructive ferocity of Grañ and his followers, directed
more particularly against churches and all objects of Christian
use, became a legend. It was also a fact of history, and to this we
must attribute the scarcity, today, of early pictures and manuscripts
and even churches—only those hewn in the solid rock or well
hidden in caves had a reasonable chance of survival. The majority
of the Christian population accepted Islam to save their lives, but
many were willing to face martyrdom instead.

The invaders enjoyed the powerful backing of the Ottoman
Turks, who were concerned at the time to extend their influence
in Arabia and along the coasts of the Red Sea. The Abyssinians
for their part received material and moral support from a small but
heroic Portuguese force under Christopher da Gama which
landed (late but not too late) in 1541. Both Turks and Portuguese
had firearms—a new element in Abyssinian warfare. For many
months the issue hung in the balance, but it was the Abyssinians
who finally prevailed; Grañ was defeated and killed near Lake
Tana in 1542. The intervention of the Portuguese had tipped the
scales and the chronicle of Galawdewos pays due tribute to these
'powerful and valorous men athirst for war like wolves and

Fig. 5   Galla sword in sheath. Length : 90 cm.

hungry for the fight like lions'. Few if any of them ever managed
to return to their homeland. They were held in great respect,
married high-born local ladies, and gradually merged with the
Abyssinian population.

The most fearful crisis in Abyssinian history had passed but the
country was left debilitated and impoverished. Exactly the same
was true of the Moslem states. Neither side was in a fit condition to
resist the inroads of the nomad Gallas who now flooded in and
established themselves—permanently as it proved—over vast
areas of the Ethiopian plateau. So the Moslem wars were followed
by the Galla wars, all exhausting, wasteful and destructive of life.

Fig. 5

The sixteenth century brought still more thorny problems,
including the arrival of the Roman Catholic missionaries whose
fortunes are briefly related in the section that follows. Another
problem was posed once again by the Ottoman Turks. In 1557
they seized Massawa, dug themselves in at Debarwa (on the
plateau, south of Asmara) and managed to scale and desecrate
Debra Damo which even Grañ had failed to do. Also they
contracted an alliance with the rebellious Bahr Negash (the
Ethiopian ruler of the sea coast and neighbouring Eritrean high-

lands). It was left to Sartsa Denghel (1563–97), last of the great
warrior kings of Ethiopia before the nineteenth century, to con-
solidate the enlarged state in the face of Galla inroads and
renewed Harari and Turkish threats, and finally to reduce his
vassal, the Bahr Negash, to submission. But the huge empire
claimed by Ethiopia since Zar'a Yaqob could not long be held
together, and disintegration was soon to set in.

Culturally, the last three quarters of the sixteenth century were
marked rather by wholesale destruction than by any new production. Except perhaps in a few quiet backwaters conditions
were far too disturbed for any creative activity. Architecture was
already in decline and its early distinction was now finally lost. But
there was no complete break in other fields of art or literature.
Their traditions remained alive, if dormant, to emerge again in
the next century.

GONDAR AND THE IMPACT OF THE WEST

Ethiopian history since the sixteenth century concerns this book
only marginally. It cannot be entirely excluded since the flourishing arts of the Gondarine period retained their unmistakable
local character; these are therefore considered in chapters VI and
VII. But the events of the last three hundred and fifty years must
be dismissed in a few paragraphs.

The region of Lake Tana, the heart of Amhara-land, had long
been familiar ground to the emperors who now and then resided
there temporarily. However, it was not until the early seventeenth
century that any king showed more than a passing interest in the
area as a seat of government: it was Susenyos (1607–32) who
first established himself at Gorgora on the northern shore of Lake
Tana. His son Fasiladas the Great (1632–67) developed Gondar,
then only a village, as his headquarters, and it was he who built
the first of the castle-palaces (huge in size by Abyssinian standards, and novel and exotic in style) for which this city is famous.
Gondar continued to be the capital during the remainder of the

seventeenth and, nominally at least, the whole of the eighteenth century. Though politically a period of decline, these centuries were culturally productive. Gondar grew into a great religious metropolis and consequently a centre of religious art and learning. Painting and calligraphy flourished under the patronage of churches, monasteries and the court.

Following the successful intervention of the Portuguese against the menace of Grañ, the Jesuit Mission (which also included Spaniards and Italians) was dispatched to Ethiopia, but with less happy consequences. The mission, which first settled at Fremona near Adua, was not fortunate in its bishops but included priests of quite remarkable devotion and perseverance. Notable among these was the Spaniard Paez who, after many years at Gorgora, crowned a career of extraordinary achievements and adventures by converting Susenyos to the Catholic faith. But when the king did public homage to an unpopular Catholic archbishop and sought to impose the new observances, his outraged people were stirred to revolt. Just before his death, Susenyos felt obliged to restore the old religion and to abdicate in favour of his son. Fasiladas led a ferocious reaction against the alien priests and all they stood for, even making agreements with the Turks who held the coast, and with the rulers of Yemen, that they should kill any Catholics attempting to enter the country. Notwithstanding these measures, the Catholic presence in Ethiopia had an enduring effect in at least one unexpected field—that of pictorial art (p. 148).

While the religious issue kept Abyssinia in ferment the monarchy enjoyed no respite from its usual preoccupations. Endless campaigns were waged against the pagans of the western marches, the unsubjugated Agaus of Lasta and Agaumidir, and the Gallas still actively encroaching in the east and south.

In the eighteenth century the rule of the Gondar kings became less and less stable or effective. After one of the more notable kings, Yasu I (the Great), had been murdered by his son Tekla

Haymanot (who was himself murdered a few years later) the credit of the monarchy itself rapidly declined. Soon the break up of the empire began, provincial governors ceasing to recognize the king's authority, and the country became a prey to intrigues and rebellions. In 1769 Yoas, the last Gondar king to attempt any independence of action, was killed by the brutal tyrant Ras Mikael, Governor of Tigrai, who had fought his way to supreme power. James Bruce, who arrived at Gondar at this time, has left a vivid and horrifying picture of the sadistic excesses he witnessed, which simply attested the breakdown of real authority.

Henceforth the monarch became a mere puppet in the hands of whatever Ras controlled Gondar at the time; new kings were appointed, dismissed and reinstated continually, frequent use being made of the reserve of royal princes imprisoned at Amba Weheni. A significant by product of the anarchic situation was the increasing influence of various Galla notables, including the first Ras Ali (Tallak Ali) who rose to be governor of Gondar. The country remained splintered until the mid nineteenth century, its main independent units being Tigrai, Amhara, Gojjam and Shoa. Gondar continued to flourish as the capital of Amhara—an area more extensive than the modern province of Beghemdir—and it is still the principal town of north western Ethiopia, playing an important part in civil and religious life.

Some outstanding Ethiopian rulers of the last hundred years, to whom the consolidation and the preservation of this unique African empire is due, can be referred to in a few words only since their times fall outside the scope of this book. There was the ill fated Kassa of Kwara, afterwards Emperor Theodore (died at Maqdala in 1868) who was the first to conceive of a reunited Ethiopia. There was John IV of the royal line of Tigrai who defended his country against the inroads of the Italians as well as the Egyptians (heirs to the ambitions of the Turks) and was finally killed fighting off the Dervishes on the Sudan border (1889).

Fig. 6   Tigrean warrior-chief showing typical Abyssinian harness, stirrup (for the big toe only), shield and lion-mane headdress (from Bent, 1893)

That mighty figure, Menelik II, king of Shoa, and then emperor (1890–1913) had been Theodore's prisoner as a child, but it was he who finally achieved the tasks of which Theodore only dreamed. Menelik extended the frontiers of the empire to the furthest confines of the plateau, or even beyond them. He frustrated the colonial ambitions of the European powers either by force or by his astute diplomacy, and he took the first steps in adapting ancient Ethiopia to the place it had to fill in the modern world.

Ras Tafari Makonnen, likewise of the Shoan line, became Regent for the Empress Zauditu in 1916, king (*Nigus*) in 1928, and Emperor, under the name of Haile Selassie I, in 1930. He has had to contend with even more complex and difficult situations than Menelik, including the disruption and discontinuity of the Italian occupation (1936–41). For over half a century he has controlled the country's destinies and ensured, in spite of setbacks, its steady advancement to keep pace with a world which has itself changed with baffling rapidity.

To these rulers the country owes its survival into the present as the longest-lived independent Christian kingdom in the world. Ethiopia may be in some ways an anachronism, but it would be a tragedy if its ancient traditions and way of life were swept completely away. Some account of these is given in the next chapter.

CHAPTER III

The Abyssinians : their Religion and their Way of Life

OLD SHOA SAMPLED

IT HAS BEEN well said that religious and secular life are inseparable among the peoples of Semitic culture. This is so true of traditional Abyssinian life that the subjects are merged in this chapter. I hope to show that the Church is the main focus of rural life, though other focal centres—the local market and the local courts—also play an important part.

To illustrate and amplify these points a map is given here which represents, on a very large scale, a fragment of the Shoan high- lands around the small town of Debra Berhan, 120 km. north- east of Addis Ababa. I lived in this district for fifteen months in 1946–48, knew the area intimately and was able to share, to some extent, the life of the people. A description of this community will typify the way of life that the Amharas have followed with little change, from century to century.

The map covers about 220 sq. km. (85 sq. miles), though the original survey extended a little farther to the west, and the statistics given below relate to the whole area. Like most of the Shoan uplands, it is a plateau lying above 2,800 m (9,000 ft) with a cool climate, except that the tremendous gorges which carve it up to the north afford warmer and more sheltered conditions.

Fig. 7

Plates 10–11

This bleak region, along with the even higher and colder district of Menz, farther north, belongs to the historic heart of old Shoa. Many names famous in Ethiopian history since the thirteenth century are associated with it, and Zar'a Yaqob made his headquarters for a time at Debra Berhan. Galla tribes invaded the plateau in the sixteenth century, pushing the Amharas into the gorges and the broken country to the east, and it was the main

concern of the Shoan princes of the eighteenth and early nineteenth centuries to regain control of the plateau. Of their two
royal residences the older one, Ankober, is 30 km. to the east of
Debra Berhan on the edge of the escarpment, while Angolala,
established about 1830, lies just off our map to the west: the old
route joining these two places is shown cutting across the area. The
great Menelik, son of King Haile Malakot of Shoa, was actually
born at Angolala, of which little now remains. At the age of
twelve he was captured by Theodore, bent on incorporating Shoa
in a newly-united Ethiopia, and carried away to the north. Later,
as king of Shoa, Menelik used Ankober for a time as his capital,
then reverted to Debra Berhan. Ever restless, like his ancestors, he
then made a temporary royal camp at Liché, a now abandoned
fort 4 km. north-east of Debra Berhan. Later, his vast southern
conquests demanded a headquarters more centrally placed. He
first moved to the high hills of Entotto far to the south-west and
finally (1889) founded Addis Ababa at the foot of those hills.

Plates 1–3

The hardy Amharas, who make their living from the windswept plateau, or from the rather cosier recesses of the gorges, are a
proud and highly individualistic people. Their hierarchical
society presents a complete contrast to that of the Negroid tribes
who inhabit the outlying parts of the Ethiopian empire to the
west and south—peoples they formerly regarded as fit only for
enslavement. The Abyssinians take immense pride in their long
history, their superior culture, and their martial prowess. Other
African (or indeed non-African) races are generally held to be
inferior. Yet I have found the Abyssinians—Amharas and
Tigreans alike—a most endearing people, whose national pride,
whose staunch conservatism and Christian piety, cannot but
impress the stranger in their midst. They are people of great
natural dignity, enhanced by the traditional *shamma*, or toga,
which is the outer garment of both sexes. They are scrupulously
polite, and a complicated etiquette is observed when persons of
unequal rank meet; yet they never show any trace of servility.

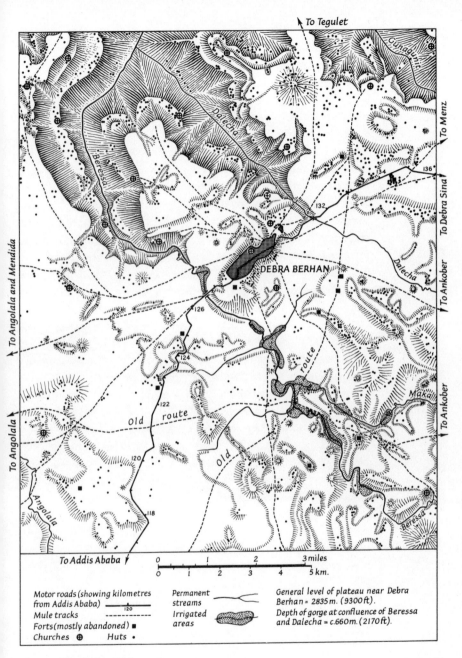

Fig. 7   The Debra Berhan area

Though often suspicious of strangers, their hospitality is generous (and their food and drink the best I know in Africa). One must admit, also, that their practical and realistic attitude to some problems of living commands respect and gives much food for thought.

One aspect of Amhara individualism is that they will not readily live together in villages. Apart from Debra Berhan itself there are in fact no concentrated settlements in the area shown on the map. Households, in this part of the country, comprise groups of stone-built round huts with conical thatched roofs, and these are widely scattered over the countryside. Since much of the plateau becomes swampy during the rains, habitations are built only on higher ground—for preference on the small secondary plateaux and rocky ridges characterizing the southern and eastern parts of the area in question. Some of these farmers held their lands by hereditary right, others were tenants of the Church or of absentee landlords and paid for their occupancy in kind. Several local headmen (*chiqa shum*) were responsible for the smooth operation of such tenancies in their respective village areas.

The population proved to be very much greater than I originally thought. Excluding Debra Berhan, it was found to average about 58 per sq. km. (150 per sq. mile)—a high figure by African standards. But its distribution was far from uniform: the plateau country as seen from the motor road was thinly populated, while a much higher density occurred near the edges of the gorges and on the habitable 'shelves' in the gorges themselves. By way of explanation, one may say that the gorge country has a less severe climate than the plateau, is better watered and produces a greater variety of crops; but there are signs that the Amhara are returning in increasing numbers to the plateau, long occupied by immigrant Galla.

The high plateau is short grass country, excellent for stock-raising but too cold for most crops. In exposed positions only barley and broad-beans flourish, but some wheat and linseed (for cooking oil) are planted, while lentils, chick-peas, etc., will survive where there is shelter. These legumes do better in the milder climate of the gorges where, in addition, *teff* (a grass-like cereal much valued for making *injera*, the local bread) can be grown. Lower down the gorges plenty of maize and millet (*sorghum*) are cultivated, also some other warm-country crops such as tomatoes, chillies, coffee and *gesho*—a shrub whose leaves are used as a fermenting agent.

Probably not more than one-fifth of this countryside is cultivable—less than this at any one time, since exhausted ground is fallowed for long periods of years and reverts to pasture. Agricultural techniques are advanced for Africa, and the plough is in universal use. Terracing is practised, especially in the gorges, and water is channeled-off from certain permanent streams to feed complex irrigation systems. (The most important irrigated areas in this tract—relied upon for a large crop of early barley—are shown on the map.)

Fig. 7

The surplus products of the country-side are regularly brought in to the big Saturday market at Debra Berhan. Local products exchanged here include all the usual cereals, butter, honey, beeswax, poultry and eggs, *gesho* and firewood (the latter being in short supply on the plateau). Earthenware vessels come from the immediate neighbourhood, splendid felted blankets and burnouses from the high sheep-rearing district of Menz further north. Traders from the eastern lowlands bring raw cotton for spinning and spices for *wat* (the hot sauce that accompanies *injera*). From desert salt-pans come solid bars of salt, often wrapped in plaited palm-leaves, which used to pass as currency. Textiles and other imported wares arrive, of course, by lorry from Addis Ababa or the north. This big regional market is not only the commercial centre but also the social centre for the neighbourhood, where news and gossip as well as goods are exchanged. It is likewise the point of contact between the governing hierarchy and the people, and was formerly the scene of royal proclamations, heralded by

Fig. 8   Chairs from Debra Damo (from Matthews)

the beating of the *negarit*—a special drum, symbol of the Emperor's authority.

If the market provides a focus for secular life, the churches serve equally essential purposes in the day-to-day existence of any rural Christian community in Ethiopia. Referring again to the region best known to me, it was found that an area of 284 sq. km. (102 sq. miles) contained no less than nineteen churches. All but three of these appear on the accompanying map, and it will be seen that the majority lie in the northerly half of the sheet, in or near the gorges. Many occupy commanding sites overlooking some wide expanse of high plateau or broken gorge country—none more dramatic than Iteghé Maryam, on a natural spur among the gorges directly north of Debra Berhan, which enjoys a fantastic panorama.

Plate 14
These churches resemble huge round huts, all except those of the town being thatched in the traditional manner. They are dedicated to those saints who, throughout Shoa at least, attract particular veneration. In view of the predominant cult of the Virgin Mary (Maryam) it was not surprising to find seven

churches dedicated to her; the next most popular were St George and St Michael with three each. Other dedications represented by one church only were the 'Covenant of Mercy', the Trinity, St John the Evangelist, and the Archangel Gabriel; while the most popular local saints, Abo and Tekla Haymanot, also had a church each.

The average number of persons served by any one church varied (according to my rough estimate) from 600 or 700 up to 1,000 or more, but it would be misleading to think of any particular church as the only place of worship for its parishioners. On the contrary, at the special festivals for the more popular saints, the people flock to a church dedicated to the saint in question; sometimes it is far away, and so they may visit five or six different churches in the course of a year. In this area the various annual festivals of the Virgin Mary always attracted large crowds, as did those of St George, St Michael, Abo and Tekla Haymanot. These were occasions of great popular rejoicing.

It was instructive, while living here in the 1940s, to discover that the ancient Church had given up none of its vital roles in rural life. Not only were those numerous churches in regular use but some of them had been set up in quite recent years to meet the needs of the gradually increasing population of the high plateau. As I wrote at the time, without the Church the social structure of the Shoan countryside would fall to pieces, and life would lose most of its variety and colour.

A corresponding description of a Tigrean village community would differ in some ways from that just given. In that northern province, which coincides geographically with the old kingdom, the land is, more often than not, communally owned. Outwardly there is a striking difference, for housing tends to be more am, bitious in the north: rectangular buildings are the rule and these are often flat-roofed, especially in the lower and warmer country. They may have good furnishings to match including, occasion, ally, chairs of attractive design. A recent journey in Tigrai has

Plates 13, 16

Fig. 8

shown me that the Church dominates the life of the community there no less than in Shoa, and monasticism flourishes as ever.

THE CYCLE OF THE ABYSSINIAN YEAR

The Abyssinians' yearly round is marked out by the succession of feasts and fasts ordained by the Church, and ordered according to the ancient calendar which survives nowhere else in the modern world (Appendix B). It must be remembered, however, that every week also has its rhythm. All Wednesdays and Fridays are fast days when no food or drink may be touched before noon and none but strictly vegetarian food for the rest of the day. Moreover, Saturdays as well as Sundays are regarded as holy days when no heavy work should be done either at home or in the fields (the same being true of all the more important festivals of the Church). There are therefore a great number of workless days, and also a great number of fast days, in the course of the year.

New Year's Day, the first of Maskaram (September 11) comes at the close of the dreary season of the heavy rains, when flowers begin to come out in millions. It is followed on the seventeenth of Maskaram by the favourite festival of *masqal* which commemorates the finding of the True Cross by St Helena. It is as much a secular as a religious feast and a great occasion for merrymaking, when warriors sing boastful chants, horsemen parade in their finest attire, and the equestrian game of *guks* may be played. On *masqal* eve, in every town, a tall pole (*damara*) is set up in some open space, and later in the day men and boys bring other long, thin poles to lean against it; this pyramid of poles is encircled three times by processions, civil and ecclesiastical. At evening the whole great pile is set alight. Since every village or hamlet has its own *masqal* bonfire the countryside that evening is full of points of twinkling light, strongly reminding any Englishman of the fifth of November at home.

In the Debra Berhan region the annual festival of Gabra Manfas Qiddus, on the fifth of Tiqimt, was always observed by an enthusiastic multitude. The little church of 'Abo' is charm, ingly situated in a grove of trees in the gorge nearest the town, not far from its *tebel* or holy water—a waterfall in the depths of the ravine below. As happened at any of these festivals the congrega, tion came and went as they pleased, but for the most part stood outside the church while the holy mysteries were conducted within. To the uninstructed onlooker the climax of the service came at the end, when the *tabot* or ark was brought out, wrapped in coloured cloths, carried on the head of a priest. As it appeared in the doorway the women raised the *ilil*, a prolonged and piercing cry of joy. At first the *tabot* remained motionless, accom, panied by several processional crosses and their attendant brightly coloured canopies, while a group of cantors (*dabtara*) performed the liturgical dance so beloved of the Abyssinians. The dancing over, a procession formed up, headed by the *tabot*, and slowly circled the church three times in a counter, clockwise direction. Finally the *tabot* was carried back into the sanctuary; all was over and the assembly broke up.

Plate 14

Plate 12

During the normally rainless months of Tiqimt, Hidar, Tahisas and Tir (October to January) the Shoan landscape gradually dries up, except where some strips and patches of bright green reveal the presence of an irrigation system. This is the harvest season, and the landscape is dotted with yellow patches, which are the threshing and winnowing grounds. At this time of year the farmers are laboriously breaking in fallow land for planting when the rains come. The matted turf is first dislodged by ploughing this way and that, then piled in small heaps to dry, and finally set alight so that it smoulders for days or weeks. This procedure kills off weeds and provides ash as a fertilizer for the next season's crops.

The great religious—and social—events of this season are the annual festivals of St Michael the Archangel on the twelfth of Hidar, and of the Virgin Mary on the twenty first of the month. On these red letter days no work is ever done; instead, all repair in newly-washed *shammas* to the local Mikael or Maryam church as the case may be. When the service is over, the *tabot* duly revealed and the *dabtaras'* dance concluded in a frenzy of emotion, many tend to linger for hours to exchange the news of the day. Meanwhile the beggars and indigent students implore, in the saint's name, the worshippers' generosity and occasionally a wandering monk or hermit will assail the laxity of the age in impassioned words and call every backslider to repentance.

About a fortnight after the western Christmas, on the twenty-ninth of Tahisas, the Abyssinian Christmas is celebrated. While not a major event of the Church calendar it makes a special appeal to young people as the occasion for a sort of inter-village hockey game known as *ganna*—the name being also applied to the festival itself.

On the eleventh day of Tir, the following month, the festival of *Timqet* commemorates at once the Epiphany and the Baptism. On the previous evening the *tabot* of every church is brought out and carried in priestly procession, with much trumpet-blowing and ringing of bells, to the local stream or pool traditionally used on this special occasion. Here the *tabots* spend the night in a tent, as they used to do when carried to the wars to bring victory in battle. Other tents are set up for the accompanying clergy, and some villagers piously remain all night in attendance, braving a hard couch of earth and a possible frost at that coldest season of the year. Very early next morning crowds begin to flock in from all sides, the *Timqet* water is blessed and sprinkled over all and sundry; some even go and splash in the stream. As the *tabot* progresses slowly back to the church on the head of a priest, crosses and canopies clustered around, the *dabtaras* keep in front, dancing as they go, with attendant drummers beating out a rousing rhythm. On the way the procession halts on some open stretch of grassland; then horsemen appear and do homage to the *tabot* by riding round it three times. This is the prelude to the dangerous and exciting sport of *guks* in which pairs of horsemen pursue each other at a frantic gallop. The leading horseman holds his shield at arm's length; the pursuer seeks to overtake him and as he does so hurls a long straight stick at the outstretched shield.

Some time during the months of Yakatit, Magabit and Miaziya (early spring in Europe) there may be light rains to mitigate the excessive dryness of the season: they rarely fail entirely in the Shoan uplands but are less reliable further north. In a favourable season there will be some ploughing and planting. This time of year, however, is chiefly marked by the beginning of the eight-week Lenten fast—the longest and most rigorous prescribed by any Christian Church.

Fasting is regarded in Ethiopia as an absolutely fundamental Christian observance and fast days, even for the ordinary layman, amount to nearly half the year. Not only is every Wednesday and Friday kept as a fast with complete abstinence until midday, but throughout Lent this applies to all week-days, though on Saturdays and Sundays eating is allowed (subject to the prohibitions of the fast) before noon. Breaking of the fast is regarded as a very serious offence, to be expiated only by appropriate penances. Even the sick cannot be exempted, when the strict attitude of the Church is upheld. We read in Walker *(The Abyssinian at Home)*:

> If the doctor says, 'Give this sick man milk with eggs and some alcohol in his broth!' the kin will say, 'Ishi! So be it!' For they will not say nay while they talk with him. But afterwards they will take counsel and one will say, 'Why should this be? Even if he dies, let him at least die pure!' And another will reply, 'If we give him this and he be cured, he can receive Penance. What matters it?' So they will dispute and some will do one thing and others another. For if they ask the Confessor, he will reply, 'It may not be! Let him not drink! Withhold! What matters it if he dies, having kept firm his religion and his purity?'

The climax of the fast comes at the end, when some men will abstain altogether from food and drink on the Friday and Satur-day before Easter; formerly there were those who abstained for three whole days and who believed that their fasting would otherwise be unacceptable to God. On Saturday night a mid-night mass is held in some churches, lasting, on occasion, well into the small hours of the morning, and pious people remain all night at church, making hundreds of prostrations as the tedious hours go by. Some time before dawn the end of the fast is made known by a signal, which may be a cannon shot in larger places, echoed by rifle fire all round the town. Now feasting begins forthwith, and for the next eight weeks until Pentecost the Wednesday and Friday fasts are not observed.

In Ethiopia the more familiar events of Passion Week are duly commemorated, with the addition, however, of the Descent into Limbo (as described in the apocryphal scriptures), which seems to have made a particular appeal to the Abyssinian imagination. Christ's visit to the nether regions, and scenes of the Devil confined by chains in his own infernal domain, appear frequently in later Ethiopian art. Easter itself, as in most Christian Churches, is considered the prime festival of the religious year. Just as palm leaves—or some local substitute—are passed round in Western *Fig. 9* churches on Easter Day, so in Ethiopia reeds are gathered and distributed round the town by the priests in solemn procession, or handed out to those who come to church, and many of the clergy and people bind them in an ingenious manner round their heads.

The first day of Ginbot (May 9) the Nativity of the Virgin Mary, *Lidata Maryam*, is the occasion for yet another special celebration. The villagers around Debra Berhan would assemble on this day on convenient hillocks or rocky ridges for a sort of village picnic—an occasion vastly enjoyed by young and old. After a general sharing round of food and drink the elders of the village gathered together, stood on the ridge facing eastwards, and one after another uttered prayers and supplications to 'Our Lady Mary' for the welfare of the village.

Later in the same month the annual festival of Tekla Hay-manot comes round, not long after which thunderstorms and an occasional whirlwind herald the approach of the rainy season. During the three months of the rains ploughmen are out con-stantly in the fields. The wide-spread mud and swollen streams make travel difficult or impossible, and the habit of attending festivals at distant churches must be suspended for a while. Nevertheless the rainy season is enlivened by its own characteristic event, the Feast of the Transfiguration (*Buhei*) which falls during the fortnight's fast commemorating the Death and Assumption of the Virgin. On this occasion the cracking of their whips by which Abyssinian boys and youths recall the night of the Trans-figuration pierces the dank and misty air like so many pistol shots.

The final month of the year—if so brief a period can be called a month—is Pagumen, which accommodates the five left-over days, or six in the year of Luke. The ending of the rains—which may be very abrupt—comes at about this time, and is greeted with general relief. So the last day of the year, the Feast of St John, comes round again, whence the phrase 'from St John to St John', i.e. 'from year to year'.

THE CYCLE OF LIFE

Every Abyssinian Christian has a soul-father or confessor who must be a priest, probably from a neighbouring church; he may know the family well and this relationship can be a very close one. The confessor's soul-children often turn to him for advice and will give him presents from time to time. He must be available for many and various services at the crucial moments of life, and, on occasion, he will indeed adopt the role of confessor. If his soul-child is guilty of working on a feast-day, or breaking a fast, of some unworthy behaviour towards neighbour or kin, he may prescribe extra days' fasting, or some hundreds of prostrations, and require donations to the Church or alms for the poor.

The confessor's services are first called upon a week after a new birth, when the baby's father asks him to sprinkle the hut with Holy Water. If the infant is male, this ceremony of purification coincides with his circumcision. The confessor, again, will arrange for the infant's baptism—boys forty days and girls eighty days after birth—and ensure that god-parents are found to play their part on this occasion. Baptism is a most complicated ceremony requiring the presence of several priests and deacons. The tying-on of the short neck-cord (*mateb*) is an indispensable part of the procedure, for this cord, from which a small cross will later be hung, is the symbol which distinguishes an Ethiopian Christian from the Moslem and the heathen.

At the baptismal service a Christian name will be given to the infant, taken from the passage of the *Synaxarium* for that particular day, but he will normally be known by the secular name already chosen by his parents. His second name will be that of his father, 'family' names being unknown in Ethiopia. After being baptised, the infants (often several will be 'raised up to Christianity' on the same day) are taken to the church to be confirmed and to receive Communion for the first, and usually the last, time in their lives. For only the priests themselves, and those few other people who have been married 'by the Eucharist', may partake of the Sacra-ment in adult life.

Marriage may take several different forms. Traditionally, it was regarded as a matter for negotiation between parents who would act through a go-between, and the principal matter negotiated was the marriage gift or 'bride price'. The appointed young couple were not consulted and might not see each other before the wedding day. Girls were considered marriageable at twelve or thirteen, or even younger; they were expected to resist their husbands on the wedding night and this resistance was com-monly overcome by force, the bridegroom's 'best man' or *mizé* assisting. To a great extent these conditions still hold good in country districts.

It is perhaps surprising that the Church, so deeply involved in most of the affairs of life, concerns itself very little with marriage. This is usually a civil contract based on the legal declaration known as the '80 Bond' (see p. 83)—made before a judge and witnesses. However, the confessors to the families do not dissociate themselves from such marriages, nor do they disapprove of them. A religious oath may supplement the brief civil ceremony, and priests are honoured guests at the long-drawn-out feasting and time-honoured buffoonery of the wedding day—or days. These civil marriages can easily be, and frequently are, dissolved. In that case any land owned by either party, or since acquired, remains the personal property of husband or wife as the case may be, and children (as well as household goods) are shared between them. The equal rights of man and wife in these circumstances reflect the high status of women in Abyssinian society.

Very few couples desire a permanent union blessed by the Church, and the priests themselves will advise caution in taking this irrevocable step, even after years of civil marriage.

If they have taken the Communion together and have become *qworabi*, there is none who can loose the bond save death; therefore few will take the Communion with a woman. . . . When a husband and wife think in their hearts to take the *Qwurban* together they will speak with the Confessor who will say to them, 'Nay, wait! Search in your soul morning and night and see if it be possible!' So they may wait more than a year.

The Church marriage when it comes is a solemn occasion. Though the couple must enter the church by their respective doors, they meet inside and, for this once only, take Communion standing together under the same *shamma*, which the husband holds. Thereafter, whenever they come to Communion, the couple must take their places separately on the men's and women's side of the church, respectively.

While marriage sanctified by the *Qwurban* is rare and greatly honoured, and marriage by the 80 Bond, or *samanya*, is normal and respectable, there are inferior degrees of matrimony. Thus a trader or soldier will usually take a *qitir* or bond-wife, the agreement being made before a judge and witnesses; such a union is readily dissolved and the property is not then shared out. A form of marriage 'by abduction' is said also to be recognized. There is nothing to prevent a man already married by the *samanya* from hiring a servant-girl (*garad*) when he has business in another part of the country and she may become his wife or concubine on a temporary basis. But if he marries a second time by the *samanya* the first wife has a legitimate grievance; if she complains to the court a penalty may be inflicted.

The clergy, so little concerned with the ordinary forms of matrimony, are needed again at death and after death. Dying men send for their confessor and ask for absolution. As soon as someone dies the women of his own and neighbouring households break into a prolonged wail. If possible the burial service takes place the same day and this service—if carried through in its entirety—includes a long series of absolutions. But if death occurs in the evening, burial will be delayed until next day. (It is noteworthy, too, that when a person dies away from home, news of the death must not be given to the relations in the evening, but withheld until the following morning.)

A variable period of mourning follows, marked by the clothes being dyed some uniform colour—any colour but white—or simply dirtied and darkened with mud, and the women shaving off their hair. But the dead are chiefly honoured by means of the so-called commemorations (*tazkar*) held 'for the drying of tears' at various intervals up to seven years after death. At the very important and obligatory commemoration held after forty days the confessor arranges for a mass to be held; there is intercession for the soul of the departed, and renewed absolutions are pronounced. Afterwards a great feast is held. As at funerals, shares of food and drink go to the priests and to officers of the Church, and the poor are not forgotten.

There is one social institution, deeply rooted among the Abyssinians, which finds no exact counterpart in other Christian societies. This is the *mahabbar*, which has been defined as a religious fraternal association. Most *mahabbars* meet once a month on one of the recurrent monthly festivals, though there are some that meet at longer or shorter intervals. Numbering from a dozen up to thirty or forty, members are chosen with care from 'men of prudent age—those who work not evil, whose nature is beauteous and calm, who anger not swiftly'. A president and deputy-president are chosen by lot, and they meet in different members' huts in turn.

These meetings both open and close with religious ceremonial. The host's confessor sprinkles the hut with Holy Water, recites prayers and blesses the food and drink provided, 'passing his cross around and over them to the four quarters'. Members on arrival prostrate themselves before the special earthenware cup or chalice; later, while all stand, each in turn will drink from it.

Mahabbar meetings are, more than anything, social occasions, to which visitors, including foreign residents, are often asked. (Women may be invited, but many women have their own *mahabbars*.) The bond between members is very strong and they seldom fail to help each other in times of difficulty or distress. It is said that even the Emperor Menelik dared not do otherwise than defer to the other brethren in his *mahabbar*, lest they should expel him from their midst.

CHURCH AND CLERGY

From the earliest times until the final break in 1958, the Ethiopian Church formed a dependency of the Coptic Church of Egypt, though it became far larger than the parent body. Its single bishop, commonly known as the Abuna or *Abbatachin* (our father) was a monk chosen by the Patriarch of Alexandria from one of the monasteries of the Egyptian desert. After a journey always long and exhausting, and usually perilous, he was obliged to spend the rest of his life, honoured but isolated and lonely, in the land of his exile. He alone could consecrate *tabots* and ordain priests. In times when the hazards of travel resulted in long periods without an Abuna, an ageing incumbent was asked to ordain hundreds of partly-trained youths, even young boys and infants, so as to provide a pool of priests for years to come.

The administrative head of the Church or *Etcheghé,* whose control extends also to all monastic communities, has since the fifteenth century been the abbot of the great Shoan monastery of Debra Libanos. Apart from the special powers reserved to the Abuna, he exercises supreme control over all the churches and monasteries of the empire. He heads a complicated ecclesiastical hierarchy among whom the provincial officers known as *liqa kahinat* (chief of the clergy) are pre-eminent. Of local Church dignitaries, the *Nebura'ed,* ecclesiastical head of Axum and the holy places of the north, occupies a position of particular honour. But every major church or important monastery has an *alaqa* as head; some of them are wealthy and live in considerable splendour.

On the other hand the ordinary priest (*qes*), while he enjoys great reverence, lives modestly and is usually a working farmer. It has already been shown that the highland Christian community lean heavily on the Church. The clergy are indispensable to the way of life of this community and some early writers were quite mistaken in accusing them of an idle, parasitic existence. However, since every church requires a minimum of two priests and three deacons, besides a sacristan *(gabaz),* a chamberlain *(aggafari)*, and a leader in singing *(mari geta)*, they and their dependents certainly form a rather high proportion of the population—probably up to ten per cent in some areas. And it has been estimated that the lands held by the Church, and used for

Fig. 9 Ecclesiastics in festive attire at Easter, with processional cross and its accompanying canopy. The brocaded, sequined robe and long hanging strips, derived from an animal-skin, may also be worn by laymen of high rank on special occasions

the support of the clergy, amount to some fifteen per cent of the arable acreage of the whole country.

The boy who aspires to the priesthood will go to a church school to be taught by a priest, a monk or a *dabtara*. Many of these students have no means of support but sleep in little grass huts erected by themselves and subsist by begging. Teaching begins with the alphabet and proceeds to a study of the principal scriptures, including the Psalms, the Gospels and the Miracles of the Virgin Mary, all studied from manuscripts written in the dead language, Ghe'ez. There is also instruction in the liturgy, and the wording of the Mass and other services must be committed to memory. At the age of about seventeen the young man is sent to the Abuna (nowadays always resident at Addis Ababa) to receive his ordination as a deacon.

If he still aims at the priesthood (but does not intend to become a monk) he must marry a maiden wife by the civil ceremony—the 80 Bond—a tie which can yet be undone. But after forty days the marriage is confirmed and rendered indissoluble in church, the couple wearing the crown (*aklil*) and taking communion together under one *shamma* as already described.

After some years as a married deacon the would-be priest will travel again to receive his final ordination from the Abuna, after which he can wear the turban of the priest. Only then can he serve in the *maqdas*, the 'Holy of Holies' of the church, and handle the *tabot*—the consecrated slab which alone confers sanctity upon the building. As a priest he will now be expert in all matters of the Church calendar and the complex ceremonial appropriate to every occasion. He will enjoy enormous respect and devotion from the public, most of whom will stop to kiss his cross on any casual meeting. He must also submit to the more rigorous discipline of the Church by observing many more fasts than the lay community—all together some 250 days in the year.

If a priest's wife dies he is precluded from marrying again—unless he quits the priesthood and becomes a *dabtara* or, as some-

Appendix B

76

times happens, takes up some lay occupation. Normally he will go once again to the Abuna or to one of his deputies, for permission to become a monk (*menoksé*). If this is granted he assumes the characteristic headgear of the monk, the *qob*. Some monks, therefore, are recruited from deacons who did not marry or from widowed priests, and these latter can still celebrate the mass like other priests. But the monastic state attracts many other categories: it is even alleged to be a refuge for debtors since a monk ceases to have any legal existence, so that his creditors can obtain no satisfaction through the courts. Some old men assume the *qob* when they begin to tire of life:

Plates 6, 122

> An old man, who has married many wives and divorced them one by one, may say, 'Henceforth it suffices me! Let the world remain lost to me! I am to turn my face to God!' and will beg the Qomos to make him a son of the qob, and the Qomos, sewing it up, will give it to him with a blessing.

Similarly many an old woman becomes a nun and wears the monastic *qob*: she 'being obliterated for God, rejects the things of the flesh and works only the work of her soul'.

The great monasteries, like those of medieval Europe, have been centres of art and learning throughout Ethiopian Christian history. There are two principal monastic orders, divided by doctrinal differences: those of Tekla Haymanot and Ewostatewos (Eustathius). The most famous of these monasteries are perhaps Debra Damo in the far north (accessible only by a rope up the rock face) and Debra Libanos in Shoa. There are, besides, various districts—Waldebba in Beghemdir, the Lake Tana islands, and Tembien in Tigrai are examples—renowned for their numerous monasteries. Most of these are to be described as loosely-knit groups of individuals rather than organized communities, for each monk pursues the ascetic ideal in his own way and is subject to little institutional discipline; some belong in

Plate 128

Plates 51–3

fact to no community at all. In these respects they seem to maintain an early Christian tradition, unaffected by the great monastic movements of the Middle Ages. In any case they enjoy high esteem with the public who admire asceticism above all other Christian virtues. Many of the monks do indeed devote themselves to fasting of a severity beyond the dreams of the ordinary mortal.

From the way of life of the non-institutional monk it is a further step to the more extreme withdrawal of the hermit or anchorite (*bahtawi*). In recent years there were still hermits living on a little-frequented hilltop not very far from Addis Ababa. Probably they still build their minute huts in lonely forest glades or among the tumbled rocks of the northern mountains. Others settle nearer to the haunts of men, using maybe a tomb-hut close to a church. For sustenance they chew roots and herbs.

> The hermit is the messenger of God, and at times will appear by night to cry aloud, 'A mighty tribulation is coming upon you! Repent!' and will disappear like a puff of smoke. He may be known by his hair, which is uncut and shaggy with butter rubbed upon it. . . . If God shows him aught in a dream, he will cry it aloud to an officer, saying, 'Such-and-such a dream have I seen! Take heed and give alms to the poor and set prisoners free!'

Lastly, a very important and peculiarly Ethiopian class of ecclesiastic are the *dabtaras* or scribes. Levine (in *Wax and Gold*) has analysed their position and their role in the following well-chosen words:

> With its characteristic forbearance towards human frailty, Amhara culture has established in the *dabtara* a religious vocation in which special knowledge is required but holiness is not expected. The vocation is thus sought by those who do not care to be bound by the strict conditions of the priesthood, or

by priests who have found these conditions too much to live with, so have been divorced and remarried.

The *dabtara*, as this quotation makes clear, is not a priest. He is not formally appointed to his office, nor does he occupy any well-defined position in the hierarchy of the Church. But, unlike many priests, he is a learned man, familiar with Ghe'ez as medieval scholars in the West were familiar with Latin, and well acquainted with the scriptures. He may be a teacher in one of the Church schools. Though barred from the *maqdas*, the *dabtara* reigns supreme in the *qené mehlet* or choir, for he is the expert in ecclesiastical chant (*zema*), and in the esoteric poetry (*qené*) which may also be sung in church. Furthermore, it is the *dabtaras* who perform the liturgical dance, to the rhythmic accompaniment of drums and sistra, without which no festival is complete.

They are also scribes, possibly expert calligraphers who add to their earnings by copying out sacred manuscripts, in which case they will also know how to prepare their own parchment, pens and ink. Some of them, too, compose amulets or spells for sale to the public, often ordered by an individual whose name will be cited in the text. They take the form of narrow parchment strips about two metres long which may be tightly rolled (and worn in decorative metal cylinders made for the purpose) or folded in zig-zag fashion with wooden covers like a small book. These amulets, which protect their owner against the evil eye, blindness and various diseases, contain magico-religious prayers invoking the deity: ostensibly Christian, they clearly have a pagan background. Other *dabtaras* are expert herbalists, willing to prescribe natural drugs against various ills. Still others make a reputation as soothsayers and sorcerers trafficking, it is sometimes said, with the powers of darkness.

The *dabtaras*, then, with their erudition, their wide knowledge and special skills, but lacking as they do the mystic and unworldly office of the ordained priest, form a kind of link between laity and clergy in this religiously ordered society. Whatever magic arts they may be thought to practice, they are highly respected citizens, whose multifarious services are indispensable to Church and people alike.

LITIGATION

It has been said that the Abyssinians take pleasure in legal disputation for its own sake, and it is probably a useful outlet for their aggressive instincts. They are proud to be fully conversant with court procedure, persuasive in pleading and eloquent in speech. The local court assembles with apparently complete informality somewhere in the open and since it is very often in session on Sundays and holidays it forms a centre of attraction, even of entertainment, to all country people not otherwise occu‐ pied. Alongside the church and the big weekly market the local court forms a third focal point of communal activity, especially in rural life. But its proceedings are bewildering to the un‐ initiated.

During the last three hundred years the *Fetha Nagast* (legislation of the kings) has been the accepted legal code of Ethiopia; in fact it is still frequently quoted. It is founded almost entirely on Roman law as modified and 'vulgarized' in the Eastern Empire during the centuries following Justinian, but there seems to have been no Ethiopic translation until the seventeenth century.

However, some characteristic legal procedures still known among the Abyssinians must have come down from much earlier times. It is noteworthy that their traditional system of conducting civil suits bears a certain resemblance to *legis actio*— the ancient Roman system discontinued in the second century B C. The most obvious feature they hold in common is that the plaintiff in each case enters a 'stake' in money or in kind which will be forfeit to the court if he loses the case. Also, both systems imply a measure of cooperation between the parties to the suit, and the procedure requires both to participate in a prescribed ritual of question and answer. Common to each system, again, is the provision for seizure of a defendant, especially a debtor—who under the old Ethiopian system might be physically tied to the creditor.

The great majority of cases arise from disputes over lands, loans and debts. In the crowded court the accuser takes his place on the judge's right hand, the accused to the left. The parties will have assembled their witnesses and themselves proposed their jurors—but the judge must ensure that these are acceptable to both sides. The accuser appeals to each juror and witness in the words, 'Have knowledge for me!' He may add, 'I trust thy neck-cord. If thou speakest for another, perish! If for God, prosper!' The accused makes his appeal by the converse formula, 'Know not against me!' etc. But litigants ignorant of the 'mouth' (i.e. of legal phraseology and procedure) may be represented by a professional advocate, either male or female. A confident accuser attempts to frighten the accused and impress the judge by entering a big stake. 'That you did so-and-so I will give an ambling mule!' (an ambling mule being the most valuable of stakes). The accused may agree and rejoin, 'Enter your stake!' But he may feel unable to accept the challenge and exclaim, 'This is not my capacity! Lower the stake for me'. And the stake may be lowered to 'a fast horse' or 'honey'.

The judge proceeds to hear the testimony of accuser, accused and witnesses. But the attention of the court will probably be diverted to side-issues—to disputes within disputes. One party accuses the other of abusive language or of incorrect procedure. The jurors must settle this side-issue before the judge can resume consideration of the main cause. Or the accused may become the accuser in the middle of the action:

The debtor will cry, 'That I gave thee the dollars I will give honey,' and counting his witnesses will defeat him, for the creditor lacks one. And they will have changed places, for the accuser stands to the right till the accused cries, 'My witnesses are greater! Turn! I shall defeat thee!' So the accuser may move aside in fear and become the accused or he may refuse and cry, 'The matter does not cause me to move!' Then the accused will say, 'That the matter does cause thee to move I will give honey!' and the accuser will reply, 'That the judges will tell me to stand in this place and defeat and strike thee down I will give two honeys!'

Many disputes that cannot be resolved by the 'small' local judge will go to the court of the 'big' judge or *wambar*, and this, or a higher court, must deal with the more important civil and criminal cases in any event. The penalties meted out by these courts range from floggings (often carried out forthwith) and terms of imprisonment down to small fines, but sentences of death (by hanging) have, in recent times, needed confirmation from Addis Ababa. Next above the *wambar*'s court comes the *chilot*, or provincial assembly, over which the governor presided with *wambars* and chiefs as jurors. There used also to be special courts in important centres for cases within the jurisdiction of the *nagadras*, the head of markets and customs. But the whole structure of the courts has been much modified since the Emperor's return in 1941.

The right to appeal to higher courts, and ultimately to the *Afa Nigus*—the emperor's chief legal officer—was a long-established privilege. *Wambars* and governors were apt to be assailed at all hours, at their homes or on the road, by aggrieved petitioners or by the family and friends of those wrongfully imprisoned; and even the emperor himself was expected, by tradition, to be equally accessible.

If a man is oppressed by the Wambar, he may place a load of stone or wood upon his head and wait by the road side or at the gate till the Governor passes. Then he will lift up his burden and cry out, 'Abiet! Abiet!' So the Governor, asking his name, will give him a 'baldaraba' or protector to recall his name to mind and will say, 'Come on the day of the Chilot!' and will wave him away.

In any description of Abyssinian legal procedures, frequent reference will be found to the *samanya*, or 80 Bond. This solemn legal undertaking, sworn on the name of the sovereign, was apparently so called because 80 dollars were—since silver dollars came into use—'the price of a life', and also the compensation awarded for serious physical injury. Those swearing by the 80 Bond need to find sureties or guarantors, who will have to pay a fine or go to prison if the swearer defaults or breaks his agreement. Sureties are in fact more easily found than might be expected— relations are loyal to their kin, and if a man belongs to a *mahabbar*, fellow members feel bound to help him, or even, on occasion, to collect the money to pay his debt or fine.

When witnesses are lacking in a case, or when an accuser insists that the accused himself should be his witness, recourse is had to the religious oath. The parties must undertake by the 80 Bond to meet at the church door on a certain Sunday before mass. The judge appoints a 'commissioner' and several jurors to accompany them and a priest must also be present. The evidence thus sworn used to be given overwhelming weight by the judges, an interesting sidelight on the immense prestige of the Church under the old dispensation, now beginning to break down.

When a debt is proved in court the debtor may undertake, by the 80 Bond, to pay up. But if no surety can be found the creditor and debtor may be linked by having their *shammas* knotted together. In earlier times, creditor and debtor were apt to be chained together and cast into prison until the witnesses of the one and the surety of the other could be found. It could also happen that debtors were kept chained for a period in the house of their creditors, who maintained them (probably on short commons, to bring pressure to bear on their friends to pay the debt) and they might even be taken away to the wars, chained to a servant. (A debtor can still occasionally be identified by a symbolic chain hanging from his wrist.)

An interesting feature of the Abyssinian legal tradition was that, in principle, any responsible citizen could be invoked as a judge at a moment's notice as, for instance, when a creditor met his debtor on the road. But another element in the community voluntarily accepts the role of peacemakers. These are the elders (*shimagile*) who may sometimes be seen grouped in earnest debate in some accustomed meeting place, devising ways and means of keeping a dispute out of court. The example of an aggrieved wife, whose husband has married a second wife by the 80 Bond, was cited by one of Walker's informants as a typical example. The elders

> . . . will finish the affair, weaving it and twisting it around; for, if they fail on the first day, they will on the morrow soften the matter and cause it to grow cold, quoting proverbs and saying to her, 'This man has done no great wrong. Do thou, my sister, abandon the affair!' and may thus with honeyed words persuade her. . . .
>
> For these ancients it is toil only, for they receive not even two or three dollars for their pains, since God created the elder to be a reconciler and a judge. Therefore do they bear labour and make reconciliations, knowing that God loves them and will reward them.

For this chapter I have drawn partly on the fascinating material collected in the early years of this century by Walker (from whose *The Abyssinian at Home* the quotations, with one exception, have been taken) and partly on my own limited experience in the 1940s, which never conflicted with his. In these times of rapid change it is sometimes difficult to be sure if old customs have remained unmodified until today, but I have generally used the present tense in the belief that the statements made are still valid, at least in country districts.

Admittedly, there have been some radical changes in the social order, notably those resulting from the series of anti-slavery laws enacted by the present emperor between 1924 and 1942. These measures sought to suppress—and did eventually suppress—a social institution as old as the state itself, and rendered a whole code of customary law obsolete. Yet the general picture, which I have tried to mirror in this chapter, shows the phenomenally conservative character of Abyssinian rural society. This immemorial way of life has appealed strongly to some outsiders who have made the country their temporary or their permanent home, and the mass of the population still cling to it with undeviating constancy.

CHAPTER IV

Architecture

PRE-AXUMITE TEMPLES

THE EARLIEST BUILDINGS of which important remains have been found in Abyssinia seem to be closely akin to south-Arabian structures of similar age—not surprisingly, since they took the form of temples probably erected by the south-Arabian colonists themselves and dedicated to the gods they worshipped.

The most impressive of these early buildings is the well-known temple at Yeha, north-east of Adua, now a village but once the principal centre of Abyssinian civilization before the rise of

Plates 19–20 Axum. Its walls, in superb dry-stone masonry, still stand high above the ground so that the German Axum expedition of 1906 was able to publish not only a plan but a well-founded recon-

Fig. 11 struction of the building. This shows a massive rectangular *cella* with upper storey and a single small window on either side. The whole stands on a 'stepped' plinth, stylobate or podium—a south-Arabian peculiarity to which the Ethiopians remained faithful for many centuries. The temple probably dates from the fifth or fourth century B C, that is, from the great days of pre-Axumite civilization when south-Arabian culture still remained a very potent and dominating influence.

The foundations of another, possibly earlier temple, of much humbler character, have been excavated by the Ethiopian Archaeological Institute at the important pre-Axumite site known as Haoulti-Melazo, south-east of Axum. This temple was a small rectangular structure with surrounding wall. Its religious character was proved by numerous associated votive offerings, mostly crude earthenware figures of cattle, while inscribed stone tablets indicated that the dedication was to Almaqah, the moon-god.

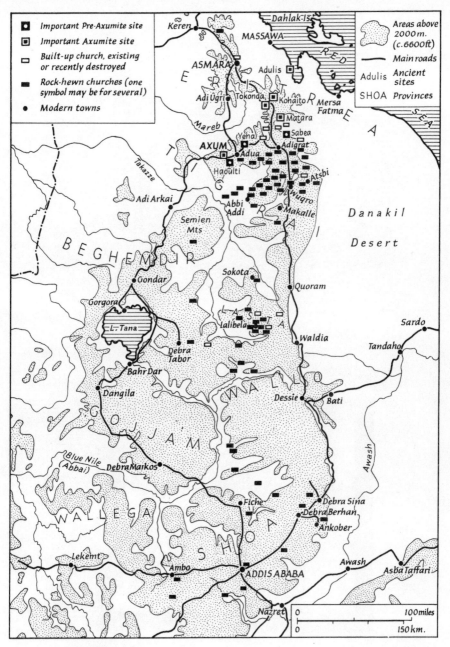

Fig. 10   Archaeological map

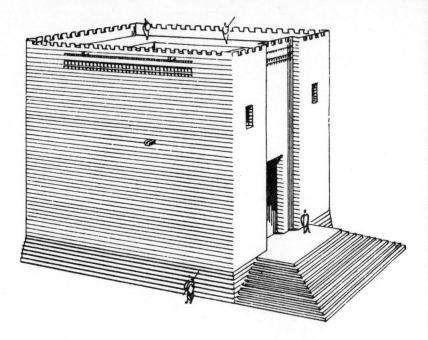

Fig. 11   Reconstruction and plan of the pre-Axumite temple at Yeha (from Krencker). Length, including steps : 25 m.

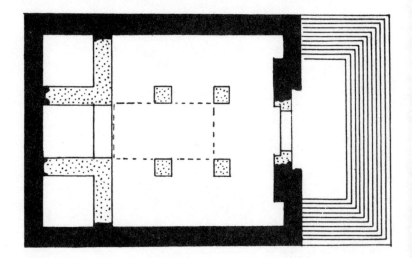

The recent non-architectural finds from Yeha, Haoulti-Melazo and elsewhere (already referred to on p. 36) provide abundant material, never before available, for reconstructing pre-Axumite civilization as a whole. So we may hope that the social setting in which such a splendid building as the temple of Yeha could be constructed and put to use will soon lose much of its mystery.

Plates 19-26

THE ARCHITECTURE OF THE AXUM KINGDOM

There is a marked discontinuity between the earlier manner of building represented by Yeha and the highly characteristic architecture of the Axum kingdom which was rising to pre-eminence during the first centuries of the Christian era. At present it is difficult to say how far these new techniques were invented locally, or whether, and whence, they may have been imported.

Our knowledge of Axumite architecture is derived from a number of sources which, taken together, permit us to form at least a partial mental picture of the great buildings of the old kingdom, though not very much remains of them above ground. Their plans and foundations were made known half a century ago by the German Axum Expedition, whose pioneer labours have been ably and successfully followed up since 1955 by the Ethiopian Institute of Archaeology.

The great stelae of Axum, also described in exhaustive detail by Krencker of the German expedition, are structures in solid stone representing multi-storeyed towers, all their architectural forms—in so far as they were visible externally—being scrupulously simulated. Only one of these towering monoliths still stands erect—it is 21 m. (70 ft) high and has ten storeys, with a false door at the base. The components of a rather taller one were transported to Rome in 1937 and erected there by the Italians. The biggest of all, which lies broken on the ground, was over 33 m. (100 ft) high and had 13 storeys; it was probably the largest single block of stone ever quarried, carved and set up in

Plates 40-2

Fig. 12

the ancient world. At the foot of each monolith is a large flat slab containing shallow circular depressions, evidently for offerings.

Fig. 12

These 'skyscrapers', culminating as they do in a pagan half-moon symbol, cannot be of later date than the early fourth century AD. No doubt they represent an architectural ideal of the Axumites rather than anything they had really erected, and one may assume that they were intended as memorials to great monarchs—perhaps as abodes for their spirits. In any case they form a record of contemporary building methods more perfect than any drawing. It is true that some of their details could not at once be interpreted in structural terms. But when the German expedition discovered, at Debra Damo, an antique church in

Fig. 12 Restored apex of the giant stela at Axum (from Krencker)

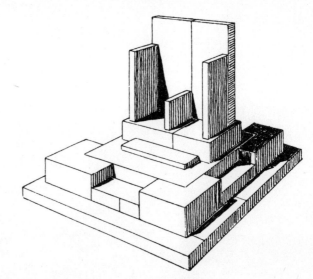

Fig. 13 Restoration of a double throne at Axum (from Krencker)

Fig. 19

which the very same features were put to structural use, the significance of every detail was revealed and their architectural character finally proved. Thus the great monoliths, in conjunction with Debra Damo, help enormously in reconstructing early Axumite architecture.

Plates 45–6

Though scarcely architectural monuments, the stone thrones of Axum must be mentioned in passing: there are many of these, all of the same general type, though a few are double. Only their ponderous bases remain; these are slotted for upright slabs which have all disappeared, but a reconstruction by Krencker is given on this page. Probably these thrones had a votive or memorial function, but one of them, surrounded by four stumpy Axumite pillars which could have supported a roof or open canopy, was used in later centuries for the coronation of the Abyssinian kings.

Fig. 13

The major buildings of the Axum kingdom all rose from a massive stylobate or podium, which in most cases is all that now remains. The podium rose in narrow 'steps' from the foundation to ground floor level—a feature these buildings hold in common with the temple of Yeha and some south-Arabian structures, such as the retaining walls of the tanks or reservoirs of Aden.

Plates 31–2

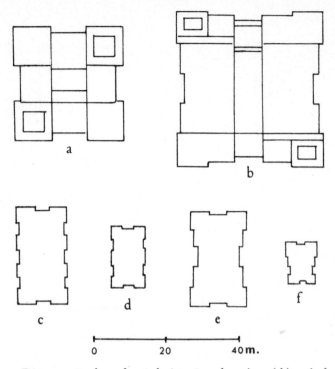

Fig. 14 Diagrammatic plans of typical Axumite palaces (a and b) and of church-types derived from them, drawn approximately to scale. Churches from Adulis (c), Debra Damo (d), Axum (e) and Kohaito (f). After Krencker

But in the times of the Axum kingdom another feature became obligatory: the buildings as seen in plan were 'indented', that is, both the podium and the wall-surfaces of the superstructure were alternately recessed and projecting—an arrangement of great importance aesthetically.

At Axum itself and at Matara on the old route to the coast the podia of many important buildings, large and impressive in their day, have been exposed. Before the advent of Christianity in the first half of the fourth century all principal buildings had as their basis a square, which might measure up to 40 m. in either direc-tion. Stairways of monumental proportions led to the main

Fig. 14

92

entrances: two types are illustrated. Clear evidence of internal **Plates 33–4**
stairways, built round a square central block, led Krencker to
suppose that there were one or more upper storeys. He also
postulated corner-towers rising a little above the general roof-
level. This feature is retained on a small scale in a surviving
built-up church (Yemrahana Kristos), and a contemporary eye- **Plate 47**
witness, Cosmas, refers to the 'four-towered palace of the King
of Ethiopia' (c.f. p. 38).

These imposing buildings, which must have been royal
palaces or mansions of the nobility, formed in some cases (possibly
in all) the nodal points of extensive architectural compositions.
They were surrounded by ranges of minor buildings enclosing
open courts, which could have been the dwellings of courtiers
and servants. The likely appearance of one such complex is
shown in the reconstruction; similar but smaller complexes have **Fig. 15**

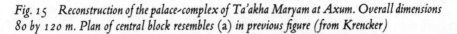

Fig. 15   Reconstruction of the palace-complex of Ta'akha Maryam at Axum. Overall dimensions 80 by 120 m. Plan of central block resembles (a) in previous figure (from Krencker)

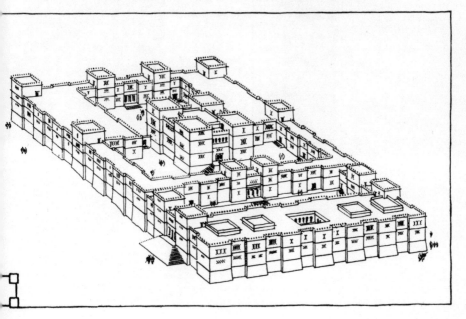

Fig. 16 Restoration of an upper-storey room of an Axumite palace. The wall structure, door and window frames and window infillings are proved by the great sculptured monoliths. Evidence for the pilasters, wooden columns and coffered ceiling comes from Debra Damo; for the frieze (as placed here just below the ceiling) from rock-hewn churches

95

been unearthed by the Ethiopian Institute of Archaeology at Matara and at Addi-Kilté just to the west of the modern city of Axum.

The ground floor of these ambitious buildings must have consisted of low, pillared halls where masonry piers or mono-lithic columns supported lintels of stone or timber. These columns were sometimes square in section with chamfered edges, some-times octagonal, sometimes elegantly fluted, but never round. Plates 35-9 They had bases and capitals which often matched and were usually either roughly cubical or 'stepped'. More complicated forms were also evolved and some of these had sockets for wooden columns. Every Axumite site provides examples of these charac-teristic forms. They can even be found lying on the ancient site of Adulis, the Red Sea port, so helping to prove that the archi-tecture of this coastal city was purely Axumite.

The upper storeys of these palaces were presumably built on the masonry-and-timber principle still exemplified at Debra Damo and described below. In any case this must have been one of the available techniques, since all its external forms are carefully copied in the storeyed monoliths at Axum, which are contem-porary with the palaces themselves. The exterior reconstructions offered by the German expedition assume that this method of building was used. I have made the same assumption in attemp-*Fig. 16* ting an interior reconstruction of a reception room on an upper floor of one of these palaces. For this purpose, however, it has been possible to utilize new evidence derived from certain rock-hewn churches in Tigrai, which seem to retain archaic features.

Sumptuous though the general effect undoubtedly is, this reconstruction illustrates the paucity of constructive or decorative forms available to the Axumites. Their architecture was wholly trabeated—there is no evidence of arches, vaults or domes at this early period. Their door and window-frame structure, used again in the frieze just below the coffered ceiling, must have lost some of its decorative appeal through too-frequent repetition. Though

the miniature-arch design shown in the window lattices certainly
existed, for it occurs in the topmost storeys of the giant stela, this
seems to have been almost the only purely decorative motif in use.
Not until centuries later do we find arched forms creeping by
degrees into the architecture—then purely ecclesiastical—of the
Christian kingdom.

Plate 44

BUILT-UP CHURCHES

Following upon the conversion of the court of Axum to Christianity in the first half of the fourth century, churches of some kind
must have been built. However, the oldest church foundations
yet known seem to be not earlier than the sixth century, and these,
while still retaining marked Axumite features (stepped podium
and 'indented' plan) are drawn out to an oblong shape. This
shows the influence of early Christian basilicas—those of Syria
in particular. A simplified basilican plan became, in fact, the
almost invariable basis of early Abyssinian church architecture.
The most remarkable survival of this style of building is the
monastic church at Debra Damo, which must be approached by
scaling a rope up one of the cliffs that surround the level summit
of the *amba*.

Fig. 14

The plan of Debra Damo (with its traditional indentations),
the transverse section and a perspective view are shown on pages
98–9. From the western porch (of later date) twin doors lead into
a low-roofed narthex, to the north of which a stairway, rising
round a square masonry block, gives access to an upper chamber.
The coffered ceiling of the narthex deserves special tribute for its
admirable panels bearing zoological motifs in relief, which may
be derived from an earlier building. Twin doors lead on again to
the nave which is divided into four bays by re-used monolithic
columns of Axumite type. On either side of the nave these
columns support lintel-beams over which runs a decorative frieze
constructed like a row of miniature blind windows; such a frieze
also runs round the sanctuary. The upper nave walls rise to a

Figs. 17–18

Plate 104

Plates 51–3

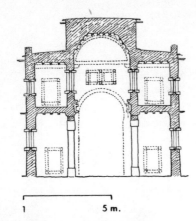

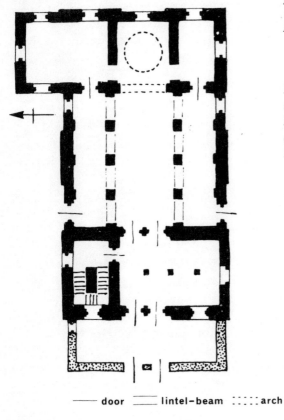

5 m.

—— door ══ lintel–beam ░░░ arch

Fig. 17 Transverse section and plan of the monastic church at Debra Damo (modified from Krencker and Matthews)

Fig. 18 Opposite: perspective view of the principal church at Debra Damo as it was in 1906 and remained up to c. 1945 (from Krencker)

height above this frieze, and formerly supported a rather complicated timber roof of uncertain date (this had to be sacrificed in
the restoration of 1948, since when the roof has been flat, and to
that extent probably more like the original Axumite roof). The
aisles are much lower than the nave and surmounted by lofts.

To the east the nave leads through a 'sanctuary arch' (the only
arch in the building) to the *maqdas*, or Holy of Holies, which is
crowned by a dome. Neither arch nor dome are properly constructed as such: the arch is composed of curved timber segments,
carved with geometrical patterns, and the dome, similarly, is
based upon a framework of curved timbers.

The walls, with their window-frames and door-frames, exhibit precisely the structure which had been emulated as early as the third or fourth century A D in the great monoliths of Axum. The technique appears to be peculiar to Ethiopia, though somewhat similar building methods have been recorded in Turkey and Pakistan. D. H. Matthews, who had occasion to dismantle a whole wall when restoring Debra Damo, has provided the accompanying drawing which shows the method of construction in detail. The core of the wall is made of small, flat, untrimmed stones set in mud-mortar. At intervals of some 50 cm. horizontal timbers are let into the inner and outer faces of the walls: in the finished wall these timbers are slightly sunk, while the masonry courses (which were always plastered over originally) project. To provide further reinforcement, small cross-members or binders penetrate the wall, being slotted down over the longitudinal timbers; these project freely outside (and some pass right through the wall, appearing internally as well). Their projecting ends are the 'monkey-heads' referred to in the literature.

Fig. 19

The figure also shows the blocks which conceal the meeting-points of the horizontal timbers and give the illusion that these are solid square beams—a device which no doubt reflects a certain scarcity of timber. Finally, the drawing indicates how the frames of windows (and of doors) are pegged together and tied into the wall. The corner-pieces of these frames pass right through the wall and are slotted to receive the longitudinal wall-beams; they therefore serve as additional binders to strengthen the whole timber framework. Their square ends, projecting at the corner of each frame, persist for centuries, not only in built-up churches but in the rock-hewn copies which they inspired, ultimately becoming the last vestige of waning Axumite influence, long after their original purpose was forgotten.

Various dates have been attributed to Debra Damo, but no one date will serve, since it represents many successive periods of building or rebuilding from early Christian times until—possibly

Fig. 19   *Axumite wall and window-frame structure based on Debra Damo.*
Two elements of the frame are shown both fixed in position and 'exploded'

—as late as the fifteenth or sixteenth century. In my own opinion much of the existing fabric could be as early as the tenth or eleventh century. In any case it remains the most perfect and the most archaic of the few built-up churches still standing in Ethiopia, with its 'indented' basilican plan, its ancient building technique, its typical door- and window-frames and frieze (all hall-marks of the Ethiopian style), its numerous lintels and its single arch in the place of honour.

The old cathedral of St Mary of Zion at Axum, destroyed in the sixteenth century, was a great five-aisled basilica, probably the most ambitious of the early built churches. We may suppose that it resembled Debra Damo in being mainly lintelled with a single arch at the eastern end of the nave, though it may possibly have had a few additional arches, e.g. at the eastern end of the aisles or the western end of the nave. It was further distinguished, almost certainly, by an external colonnade, a feature perpetuated in some rock-hewn churches.

Plate 59

The distribution of the more important built churches of early date, either surviving or recently destroyed, can be seen from the map. One that formerly existed in Asmara disappeared about 1920. Of others in Eritrea, Aramo survived until the 1940s and Debra Libanos until about 1960. Further south a new discovery has compensated in some degree for these tragic losses: Debra Selam near Atsbi in Tigrai is an exquisite miniature church, partly rock-hewn and partly built-up, immured in a rock-shelter among picturesque sandstone cliffs.

Fig. 10

Plates 47-9

The fascinating district of Lasta claims at least four such churches, all protected from the elements in great caves. Of these, Yemrahana Kristos (a day's journey north of Lalibela) is the most perfect and perhaps the most striking with its conspicuously striped walls (lacking, however, in 'monkey-heads'). The interior, too, where arches have supplanted all lintels, is the richest we know, with an elaborate and beautiful nave roof, a dome over the sanctuary, and a wealth of carved and painted detail, much of it apparently of Islamic derivation. This church is of great architectural importance since, whether or not it actually ante-dates them, it embodies traditions which powerfully influenced the rock-hewn churches of Lalibela.

East of Lalibela, in the mountain-mass of Mekena, two charming toy churches stand in their respective caves, as does Jammadu Maryam still further east. Far to the south-west of Lasta in the direction of Debra Tabor (Beghemdir), is the curious, isolated example of Betalehem, where the ancient church is concealed inside a round one, of later date, with thatched roof. None of these can be dated, but I suspect they are all more recent than Yemrahana Kristos, which is itself some centuries younger than the antique prototype represented by Debra Damo.

Plate 50

THE ROCK-HEWN CHURCHES

The now famous rock-churches of Lalibela were first made known to the outside world by Alvares, the chaplain and chronicler of the Portuguese embassy of the 1520s. However, few foreign travellers penetrated to that inaccessible region during the next three hundred years. Only since 1960 has this ancient town with its remarkable monuments been made accessible to the ordinary visitor—in the dry season at least. At the same time it has at last become clear that there is another, perhaps even more important, concentration of rock-hewn churches further north, in the province of Tigrai. Indeed, so many have been located there in recent years that the total number known in the country has at least been trebled, and no doubt many more remain to be found. It is noteworthy that the great majority of these are still in use and have obviously been well known to the local populations ever since they were excavated some time in the Middle Ages.

These rock-churches seem to possess no style of their own but to be more or less accurate copies of those built as usual. According to tradition, the Abyssinians invoked the aid of foreigners—

Fig. 20 Frieze and coffered ceiling at the western end of the nave at Adi Qasho

apparently refugee Christians from Egypt—to assist in the task of hewing them out of the rock. This may be true, and there are certainly signs of Coptic influence in some decorative details of early Abyssinian architecture (see p. 160). But the significant fact remains that the rock-churches continue to follow the style of the local built-up prototypes, which themselves retain clear evidence of their basically Axumite origin.

Churches were being hewn from the rock over a long period, from as early as the tenth to as late as the fifteenth or even early sixteenth century, after which the Moslem and Galla wars brought any such activity to an end. But the period of their invention and first great expansion seems to coincide with the rule of the Agau kings who already occupied the throne towards the end of the tenth century and retained it until 1270. The fact that the pagan Agaus already worshipped in caves may possibly

Fig. 21   Western façade of the rock-hewn church of the Redeemer at Adi Qasho in its original condition

explain their predilection for rock-hewing when they came to require churches.

Among rock-excavations known to me only one appears to be a deliberate imitation of an early Axumite church; this could be one of the first attempts to carve churches from the rock and could date from the tenth or early eleventh century. I refer to the three-bayed basilica of Medhane Alem (the Saviour of the World) near the village of Adi Qasho north of Wuqro in Tigrai. Like Debra Damo it is entirely lintelled except for a single arch leading to the sanctuary. Its ceilings are uniformly flat, and *Fig. 20* decorated with reliefs which imitate wooden panelling and other roofing techniques. Entering the church from the west one passes between great rectangular columns cut from the cliff-face in which the church is sunk. They form a massive colonnade *Fig. 21* such as one imagines some Axumite churches possessed: un-

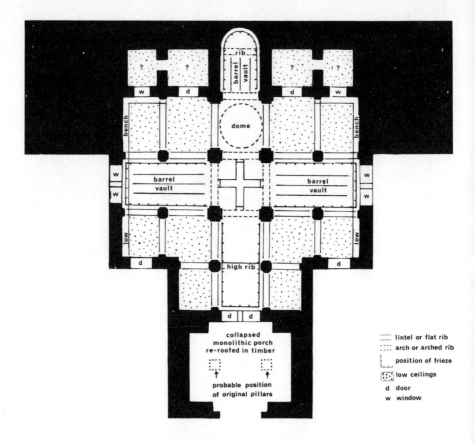

Plates 60–2

fortunately the spaces between the columns have been subsequently blocked, but the line drawing above shows their original appearance. The colonnade forms one side of a vestibule or narthex which has coffered ceilings, and an Axumite frieze runs along the walls just below these ceilings. A frieze also adorns the nave-walls of the church proper, which are supported on big clumsy piers. In view of its completely flat ceilings this church represents a stage even more archaic than Debra Damo.

The next type of church to be mentioned is represented by three examples in Tigrai: Cherqos Wuqro on the main north road, Abreha Atsbeha west of that road and Amba Mikael, which is

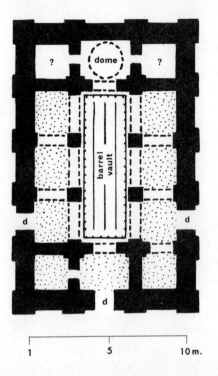

Fig. 22 Plans of rock-hewn churches: left, Abreha Atsbeha, 'semi-detached',
cross-in-square; above, Amanuel at Lalibela, monolithic, basilican

carved out of a mountain-top some way to the east. Unlike other
early Abyssinian churches, they have a complicated non-
basilican cross-in-square plan and a well-marked transverse axis.
Each church is provided with a western porch or entrance-lobby.
The arms of the cross, which do not stand out on the plan, are
evident enough in the churches themselves since they rise high,
may be surmounted by long barrel vaults, and are further defined
by a circumambient frieze. The middle point or crossing is
distinguished by imitated crossed beams which may rest on
brackets, while the dome which one might expect to find in this
central position is displaced one bay further east. The eastern arm

Fig. 22

Fig. 26

107

terminates in a semi-dome. No built-up prototypes of these churches are known to have survived in Ethiopia. However they are apparently a simplified version of a very early cruciform church plan which is known from the Christian sites of Gerasa (Jerash), Ephesus, and Salona in Dalmatia.

What points to an early date for these remarkable excavations is the absolutely correct use (alongside novelties like vaults and domes) of Axumite-type columns and capitals supporting lintels, which in turn bear friezes of the traditional type. Moreover, though so sophisticated in plan and workmanship, they are not yet monolithic, only their western half being freed from the parent rock. I believe them to be earlier than Lalibela, probably eleventh or twelfth century.

Lalibela itself with its dozen rock-churches is so named after the early thirteenth-century Zagwé king who, according to a very strong tradition, himself created them. The date is plausible enough, though the time spent on these multiple excavations must have been far longer than the few decades allowed by the legend: more probably the work extended into the fourteenth century. Lalibela is a veritable labyrinth where rock-churches jostle one another and rise one upon another, where some stand free and others remain subterranean, where the ground is riddled with trenches, crypts and tunnelled passages.

Plates 56–8   The four most ambitious of the Lalibela churches have attained the ultimate in rock-church design: they are virtually free-standing, being attached to the surrounding rock only by their bases. The excavators of these monolithic shrines first isolated huge blocks of rock by digging out deep trenches around them. These blocks were then carved into the forms of a church both outside and inside, the work proceeding from the top downwards. One is amazed at the technical skill, the material resources and the continuity of effort which such vast undertakings imply.

Fig. 22   Architecturally, these churches tend to conform to the basilican plan complete with western narthex and triple eastern sanctuary.

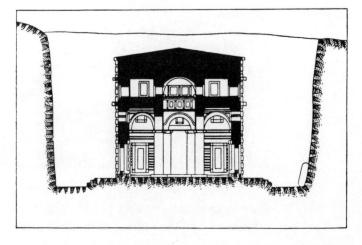

Fig. 23   Transverse (N-S) sections of two monolithic churches at Lalibela, standing in their excavated courtyards : top, Amanuel (Emmanuel), three-aisled, with lofts ; below, Medhane Alem (The Redeemer of the World), five-aisled, with external colonnade, but no lofts (after Monti della Corte)

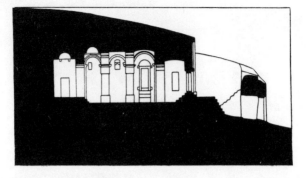

Figs. 17, 23

Plates 57, 63, 97

Plates 47, 58

Two of them follow, with great fidelity of detail, the tradition represented by Debra Damo as modified at Yemrahana Kristos. That is to say they have the same cross-section as Debra Damo, with lofts over the aisles, but, as at Yemrahana Kristos, arches have now taken the place of lintels. A simulated barrel vault surmounts the nave and a dome the sanctuary, friezes are perfectly traditional and doors and windows also follow the old Axumite pattern. Of these two churches Maryam (St Mary), though outwardly plain, contains complicated relief decoration inside, the geometrical patterns in the soffits of the arches being directly copied from wooden models. The other church, Amanuel (Emmanuel) even imitates, both inside and out, the timber and masonry courses of the old building technique, as had already been done on the monoliths at Axum; here, however, the 'monkey-heads' are omitted as in the built-up prototype at Yemrahana Kristos.

Reverting to Maryam, it possesses a very spacious court leading, at its western extremity, to a raised passage which forms, as it were, the roof of lower excavations, and these ramify below the western end of the Maryam court itself. They include the church of St Michael and, alongside it, the Golgotha chapel leading in turn to the crypt of the Trinity. The last two chambers contain over-life-size mural figures of saints in high relief, framed in blind

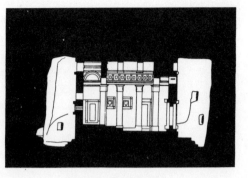

Fig. 24 Longitudinal (W-E) sections of two partially isolated rock-hewn churches: left, Bilbala Cherqos, with three worked façades (cf. fig. 22a); right, Abba Libanos, Lalibela, which has four worked façades but is joined to the cliff above (after Monti della Corte)

0   2   4   6   8   10 m.

arches (they show kinship with Coptic art, see p. 160). Close by is Medhané Alem ('Saviour of the World'), a five-aisled basilica and the largest of all the monolithic churches, measuring 33.5 m. from west to east. Its rows of gaunt columns and ponderous round arches are reminiscent of some great crypt of a western cathedral. It is completely surrounded by tall free-standing square pillars which, at their summits, join the overhanging eves of the roof. This peristyle may have been inspired by the old cathedral of Axum, as suggested above (p. 102), and it certainly inspired, in turn, the similar feature at Ghenetta Maryam, an outlying monolithic church of later date in Lasta.

Fig. 39

Fig. 23

Plate 59

Of the five monolithic churches in this area St George remains to be mentioned. It stands by itself in a deep pit so that, on approaching, one first sees the roof with its nested Greek crosses in bold relief. Alone among the Lalibela churches its plan is non-basilican but takes the form of a cross, both outside and inside; yet it has little in common with the 'cross-in-square' churches of Tigrai. Its affinities are enigmatic, but it seems to have been subject to new influences and so to be the latest in date of the principal churches in the Lalibela complex.

Plate 56

Lasta and neighbouring districts provide examples of various types of rock-church less advanced than the monolithic. Although I do not believe that any of them ante-date the masterpieces of

Fig. 24

Lalibela, they nevertheless illustrate logical stages in the evolution of the free-standing rock-church. Thus Abba Libanos, cut into the base of a cliff in Lalibela itself, is not quite monolithic since it merges with the rock-face above; yet its four sides are all isolated and a dark passage surrounds it. The rock-church near Sokota in Waag, farther north, is of similar design with all its façades exposed. There are also those which, after the manner of the cruciform churches in Tigrai, project from the rock to the west only and have been described as 'semi-detached': Bilbala Cherqos is of this type. Others are less ambitious with but a single worked façade, the rest of the church being sunk in the rock. Others, again, are simply internal excavations whose presence can only be detected outside by a few holes in the rock-face. An example of this last type, notable for its exceptionally fine set of wall-paintings, is Yadibba Maryam in Daunt, a remote district to the south of Lasta.

Plates 84–5

Lalibela lies far to the south of the original motherland of the Axumite style. The force of this ancient tradition was slightly attenuated here, and some mannerisms developed which the purist might regard as architecturally incorrect. This is illustrated by the treatment of capitals. For instance at Abba Libanos—which perpetuates an early church-type with lintelled nave—the capitals are not properly Axumite but a peculiar reduplicated type unknown outside Lalibela. Similarly, at Maryam, Amanuel and Medhané Alem a new attitude to the 'bracket-capital' can be observed. The original practice was to use a bracket or corbel only where actually needed to support an arch or lintel. If several such brackets were required at the same level on a pillar they presented the appearance of a capital; but they might equally well be set at

Fig. 25

different levels or, lopsidedly, in threes (an arrangement also common on piers—but not simple columns—in the Romanesque and Gothic). In these Lalibela churches we find, however, that a capital which would traditionally be three-bracketed (as at Yemrahana Kristos) has a fourth bracket added, which has nothing to support. Logic has been sacrificed to symmetry, and these capitals are now thought of as indivisible units, as in most western architecture.

After rock-excavation had reached its peak in Abyssinia— apparently in the twelfth and thirteenth centuries—many more churches continued to be hewn from the rock and the areas where such excavations were attempted became widely extended, as the archaeological map shows. The great majority of rock-churches *Fig. 10* in Tigrai seem to me to belong to this later period, dating probably from between the late thirteenth and the fifteenth century, if not still later. Probably the great southward extension of this archi- tecture, of which more and more evidence is being accumulated, took place during the same period, or the latter part of it. This is of great historic interest since the presence in Shoa of these sanctuaries (even south of Addis Ababa) proves the existence of Christian communities far to the south of the old confines of the kingdom in comparatively early times.

The known outlying groups of later rock-churches are of minor architectural importance. But in Tigrai, closer to the

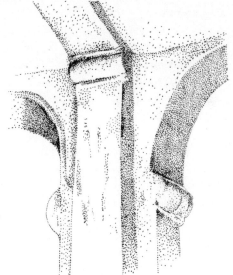

Fig. 25 Logical employ-ment of corbels at two levels in the rock-hewn church of Barka near Atsbi, Tigrai

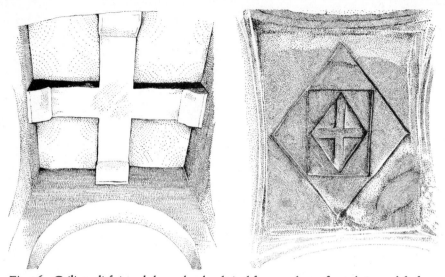

Fig. 26   Ceiling reliefs in rock-hewn churches derived from wooden roofing techniques : left, from Abreha Atsbeha, Tigrai ; right, from Sokota in Waag, Wallo

original source of the style, there are interesting later developments. We see no more of the complicated cruciform layout described earlier, but basilican churches abound. They are characterized by the enrichment of their ceilings with saucer-domes and, more than ever before, with designs based upon old roofing techniques.

Fig 26

The most popular of these designs imitates the device whereby a square was progressively reduced to smaller and smaller squares by diagonal timbers placed across the corners. Arches are multiplied as in Lasta but some of these churches also retain the primitive lintel, especially in the western narthex or vestibule which is almost always present. Some still have friezes of the old Axumite type, which however come to be supplanted by a miniature blind arcade.

Among many notable examples of these later churches three must be mentioned here. Wuqro Maryam in the district of Amba Sanayt (south-west of Adigrat) has a very tall nave with lintels

Fig. 27

and friezes and the most extensive known set of ceiling reliefs;

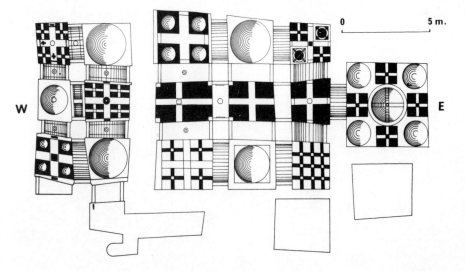

Fig. 27 Ceiling reliefs of the rock-hewn church of Wuqro Maryam in Tigrai, as viewed from below (from Mordini)

it was fully described in 1939 by Mordini, who proved that it could not be later than the early fourteenth century. The monastic church of Abba Yohanni is a most impressive domed excavation high in a cliff-face west of Abbi Addi (Tembien). Debra Tsion, cut into a mountain top of red sandstone in Gheralta (north of Makalle) has richly adorned domes rising on pendentives, giving a strongly Byzantine effect; there is evidence dating it to the beginning of the fifteenth century. All these are, by rock-church standards, of imposing dimensions, reaching an interior height of 9 m. (30 ft).

Plate 65

Many of these churches contain one or more monolithic 'altars' and these vary in design. As a rule they cannot be properly seen, owing to the inaccessibility of the sanctuary. The following sketch shows, however, a pleasing example which I was able to record in an abandoned church in Tembien. For comparison, an earlier solid stone altar from Lalibela is also shown; this is evidently copied from a wooden, portable prototype.

Fig. 28

115

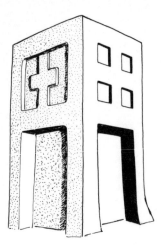

Fig. 28 Monolithic altars from rock-hewn churches: above, crypt of the Trinity, Lalibela; right, Wolegheso Yesus, Tembien district, Tigrai. Height: c. 1.5m.

OTHER CHURCHES—NORMAL AND ABNORMAL

While describing the important monuments of Ethiopian architecture I have left the more modest churches of the country-side out of account. Yet these constitute the vast majority and really form part of the Ethiopian landscape (an idea of their distribution in a small area is given by the Debra Berhan map).

Fig. 7

Round churches with conical roofs are universal in Shoa, and in the Christian south and west generally, and like ordinary round huts may be built of 'wattle and daub' or of stone. Many churches of this form, or its octagonal derivative, have been built even in the north in modern times. Though so abundant in Ethiopia today—they seem to have become more and more popular in the last few hundred years—round churches cannot be

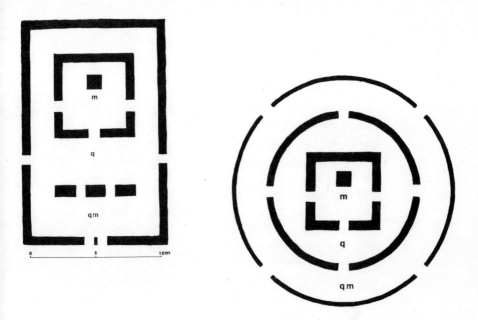

Fig. 29   Types of modern rectangular and circular church plans with isolated sanctuary.
    m = maqdas, (Holy of Holies); q = qiddist; qm = Qene mehlet

of very early origin. The characteristic country church of Tigrai Plates 13, 14
and Eritrea, where ancient traditions live on, is rectangular and
solidly built in masonry, with a flat roof, through which the top
of the sanctuary often rises to a higher level. Nearly always, in the
north, there is a set of two or three stone bells or 'phonoliths'
suspended in a wooden framework close to the church.

The accompanying diagrammatic ground-plans indicate the *Fig. 29*
normal layout of modern Ethiopian churches. Whether round or
rectangular, they have lost all trace of the old basilican plan, even
though other details are often archaic. The *maqdas* is normally
square and stands by itself. It contains an altar-slab (*tabot*) or more
than one of these, kept in a wooden altar-chest (*manbara tabot*)
and this part of the church can be entered only by the clergy. The

117

inner ambulatory is the *qiddist* used by communicants at mass. A second, outer ambulatory (if present) or any available space to the west will be the *qené mehlet* used by the *dabtaras* and accessible to anyone (p. 79). Except for the *maqdas*, the Holy of Holies, these different spaces are not always very clearly defined—even less so in the early basilicas. I am not myself convinced by the theory that they reflect the three-fold division of the Hebrews' temple.

In the more rugged highland regions, especially in Eritrea, Tigrai and Wallo, many other churches can be seen which are neither round nor oblong. They cling to the cliffs or seem wedged into caves and fissures among the rocks. The extant buildings may or may not be ancient—though some of these sites may well have been sacred places even before Christian times. Some have their interior spaces enlarged by excavation but they cannot qualify as rock-hewn churches and I have made no attempt to show them on the archaeological map. These sanctuaries among the rocks are not serious monuments of architecture but they are memorable for their unexpected forms and their often extraordinary setting among the mountains and gorges of the northern highlands.

Plates 66–7

CHAPTER V

Literature

IT HAS ALREADY been seen that the early colonists from southern Arabia brought with them to Ethiopia not only a Semitic language strange to Africa but also the Sabean or Himyaritic syllabary in which this language could be written. Although subsequently modified and improved, this archaic but not unpractical alphabet remains in use to this day, as do the three languages descended from the original Ghe'ez or Ethiopic. This illustrates the persistence over more than two thousand years of the Abyssinian literary tradition—a phenomenon otherwise unknown in Africa, since other early scripts and languages, notably those of Egypt, fell out of use and were forgotten long before the dawn of modern history. Moreover, Ethiopia has long enjoyed, thanks to the Church, a certain degree of popular literacy.

Yet, in spite of the immemorial antiquity of the written word among the Abyssinians, its documentary tradition is sadly discontinuous. Of the early inscriptions, which have so much historic and even some literary interest, few are later than the fourth century, probably none later than the ninth. From the next four hundred years scarcely a document, whether on stone or parchment, has survived. Some literary activity must have continued during the period of the Agau monarchy, but architecture rather than literature was their main concern.

With few and rather uncertain exceptions the oldest manuscripts known to survive date from the thirteenth century. All are written on parchment, the pages being marked out for margins, columns and text by faint lines scratched with a pin. In this and other ways they closely resemble western medieval manuscripts. Many of these early books are written in a very beautiful character, and some of the Gospels, from the fourteenth century onwards,

contain illustrations of exceptional interest (see Chapter VI).
Thereafter, in spite of interruption during the troubles of the
sixteenth century, the art of the Ethiopian scribe, and the art of
the miniaturist, were both maintained continuously, being fos-

Plates 29, 30   tered by the monasteries and by the royal court. Calligraphy in
particular was the glory of Abyssinian book production,
reaching a second peak of elegance (and its grandest scale) in the
eighteenth century, after which it declined.

We are therefore concerned exclusively with a manuscript
literature. No printed books came into general use until late in the
nineteenth century. Even then mass-produced books failed to
command the reverence accorded manuscripts, which are still
prized possessions, and essential equipment for the clergy.

Fig. 30   Sometimes the more portable volumes (especially selections from
the Psalms) are provided with a leather case, or even a double case,
and are worn slung from the shoulder by itinerant priests and
dabtaras, or by monks on pilgrimage.

The prose literature of the Abyssinians consists in large part
of the scriptures translated from Greek or Arabic sources,
including many works regarded in the west as apocryphal. It
also includes a vast hagiographical literature, celebrating the
lives and acts of local saints, besides those of wider renown; also
a certain number of theological books. The supply of these
religious texts, many of them indispensable for liturgical use in all
Abyssinian churches, was maintained for the most part by the
monastic scriptoria. Then there is the secular literature, mainly
royal chronicles, composed and written out at court. In addition
to prose works there is a popular and more original genre which
partakes rather of the nature of poetry. Here again we may distinguish a religious category—hymns and verse for use in church
—and a secular category, including martial chants and songs in
honour of great men.

All these books were written in, or translated into, the aboriginal
Ghe'ez language. This was regarded as the proper vehicle for all

literary compositions, just as it continued to be the language of the liturgy, long after it ceased to be generally understood. Not until the seventeenth century was even a chronicle composed in Amharic, which was becoming by degrees the most widespread language of the people. For this reason alone nothing like a popular literature could emerge. This only became possible as a result of social changes and the introduction of the printing press in very recent years.

Fig. 30 A pilgrim's holy manuscript with inner and outer leather case and shoulder strap. When the narrow thong is pulled, the book slides out. Overall length : 20 cm.

EARLY TRANSLATIONS FROM THE GREEK

That great early scholar—Ludolf—was the first to maintain that the Ethiopic version of the Old Testament must have been translated from the Septuagint of the Greeks. Later scholars have confirmed his view. It is also generally agreed that the New Testament was taken from a Greek text, namely the text used by the Syrian Christians in the Patriarchate of Antioch, but the Syriac version may also have been consulted. It is known that Syrian monophysites came to Ethiopia as refugees from Byzantine persecution in the fifth and sixth centuries—among them the 'Nine Saints' who played a great part in the spread and con-solidation of Abyssinian Christianity. These immigrants may well have included learned men who devoted themselves to the great work of translating the scriptures. Both Old and New Testaments were revised in much later times under the influence of the Christian Arabic text adopted by the Coptic Church, to which the Abyssinian Church had long owed allegiance.

Some other scriptures derived by the Abyssinians from Greek sources were always regarded as authentic in Ethiopia, though rejected as non-canonical in the West. Such are the Book of Jubilees, the Apocalypse of Esdra, the Ascension of Isaiah, and the Book of Enoch (for most of which the Ethiopic version is the only known surviving text). In addition, the lives of the Desert Fathers, St Anthony and St Paul the Hermit, became available; also the Rule of St Pachomius, a treatise fundamental to the development of Ethiopian monasticism. Among theological works the *qerlos* ('St Cyril') is important; besides extracts from the saint's own writings, it contains quotations from other Greek Fathers of the Church. It is a polemical work, supporting the monophysite doctrine against the errors of Nestorianism. Still another book translated at this early period was the *Physiologus*, that famous work of natural history, intended rather to edify than to inform, in which nearly every plant or animal becomes a symbol, and every story points a moral.

During the five or six centuries following the era of the Greek-Ethiopic translations, the Abyssinians remained, in spite of political upheavals, intermittently in touch with their mother Church in Egypt. Since Coptic literature was flourishing during this period one might expect to find Ethiopic translations taken straight from the Coptic, but there is no proof that any such exist. The fact was that Ethiopic literature—though there cannot have been a complete break in its tradition—stagnated during the very period when the Coptic output was most prolific. When, after hundreds of years, the Abyssinians were at last ready to absorb new material into their literature, Coptic had been superseded by Arabic as the language of the Egyptian Christians, and the scriptures had all been made available in Arabic versions.

THE GREAT AGE OF ETHIOPIC LITERATURE: FOURTEENTH AND FIFTEENTH CENTURIES

A great literary revival began in the fourteenth and continued into the fifteenth century, being fostered by two notable monarchs: Amda Tsion I (1314–44) and Zar'a Yaqob (1434–68). Many new Ethiopic translations were made from the Christian Arabic versions then in use in the Coptic Church, and some original books were produced. This considerable output included both prose and poetry. As in the case of the earlier literature, we notice an overwhelming preponderance of religious works, especially the Lives and Acts of the Apostles, saints and martyrs. The *Senodos*, a book of the canons of the Coptic Church, was also issued at this time.

Most important of all was the great *corpus* of saintly lore known as the synaxarium (*senkesar*), a calendar of saints with sections to be read in church on every day of the year. It normally occupies four huge manuscript volumes, each covering three months of the year. Although this was at first simply the synaxarium of the Copts, the book underwent gradual 'acclimatization' in the

Abyssinian scriptoria: they enriched it with more and more lives and acts of local saints while introducing copious references to the festivals peculiar to the Abyssinian Church. The book first made its appearance in an Ethiopic version towards the end of the fourteenth century; it became immensely popular and stimulated the writing of various books on local saints during the next hundred years.

As an example of an apparently original composition of the late fourteenth century we may mention the 'Book of the Mysteries of Heaven and Earth'. It shows that the practice of religious reverie was not unknown in Abyssinia—though doubtless confined to a few rare 'illuminati'. This extraordinary work presents the revelations of an angel as made to the author, the monk Yeshaq (Isaac). His mind was perhaps prepared by such passages of scripture as II Corinthians 12, 1–4. Yeshaq's musings are expressed in complex and mysterious symbolism which only the initiated were expected to understand. In a passage quoted by Cerulli, we read of the 'white birds'—all female, and fertilized by the sun—which dive down to the depths of the ocean and there give birth, firstly to their own young, then to various numbers of pearls, finally to a single pearl of surpassing beauty. (The symbol of the Pearl was already popular in eastern Christian literature, which adopted it from the *Physiologus*; but the pearl's mystic significance was transferred, in Abyssinian usage, from the Redeemer to the Virgin Mary.)

Several religious works, including the 'Book of Light' and 'Book of the Nativity' are attributed to that remarkable monarch, Zar'a Yaqob, himself, though it seems more likely that they were written by ecclesiastics of the court under the king's direction. The purpose of these books was to reinforce the authority of the sovereign and to combat the current tendency towards heresy and pagan practices. These books are full of exhortations and dire warnings to the people. They illustrate the personal intervention of the king in ecclesiastical affairs, and are interesting as belonging

via Christian Arabic versions, were translated into Ethiopic
towards the end of the fifteenth century. In subsequent art he is
shown mounted on a white horse, and spearing the dragon, *Fig. 33*
usually not far from the two local saints just mentioned.

Of these books of saintly lives and miracles, none is more
characteristic of the country, none illustrates better the Ethiopian
genius for absorbing and transmuting foreign elements, than the
Ta'amra Maryam—the Miracles of the Virgin Mary. Cerulli, Plates 91-2
who has made an exhaustive study of this fascinating work,
traces its origins back to medieval Europe, where collections of
these miracles were made from the mid⁄twelfth century onwards
by such authors as William of Malmesbury and Gautier de
Coinci. They were based on legends and miracles associated with
some of the great European pilgrimage centres—Rome, Toledo,
Santiago de Compostella, Laon, Chartres, Rocamadour,
Mont Saint Michel. The *Miracles* were first disseminated in
France and the Anglo⁄Norman kingdom, but were translated
in the course of time into almost every European vernacular, even
as far afield as Iceland. New editions both in prose and verse,
enlarged and amended according to local resources and local
taste, went on appearing until the fourteenth century, and con⁄
tinued thereafter to inspire poets and artists.

From our point of view the crucial turning⁄point in this
literary saga was the translating of the *Miracles* (some time in the
twelfth century, probably from a French version) into Arabic.
This translation passed from Palestine to Syria and to the Copts
in Egypt, gathering new material all the time. When this already
multifarious collection had been translated into Ethiopic at the
very end of the fourteenth century, there were of course further
accretions, some based on real local events. The Ethiopic
versions normally include the 'canon' of thirty⁄three officially
recognized miracles together with a variable number—even as
many as 283—of additional ones, born of the fertile imagination of
successive editors.

From the fifteenth century onwards the *Miracles* were read regularly in churches on all the numerous festal days dedicated to the Virgin Mary, and they came to be regarded, in the credulous eyes of the Christian community, as equivalent in importance and authenticity to the Gospels themselves. Many copies of the book include a preliminary section on the 'Covenant of Mercy', inspired by the apocryphal narrative of the Pseudo-Melito. It is well placed here, for the thought lying behind these miracles is unintelligible unless one allows for an unquestioning faith in the 'Covenant', whereby Christ promised his Mother: 'Every soul that calleth upon thy name shall not be put to shame, but shall find mercy and consolation and succour and confidence.' The Virgin Mary, therefore, came to be regarded as chief among the heavenly champions of all erring souls. The influence of this belief is seen in an Ethiopian's account of the fate of good and evil souls, as recorded by Walker in *The Abyssinian at Home*:

When a man dies, Michael clasps him by the right hand and the Devil by the left, and thus they ascend to heaven. There the two argue before God as at a law-suit, the Devil crying, 'This soul is mine! Continually it worked sin and evil!' But Michael may answer, 'It is not thine but mine!' and together with Mary may cry, 'Bring forth the scales! Let us weigh the soul!' For the man may have eaten and drunk monthly of the *tabal* and *tadiq* of Michael to honour him, or when a beggar stretched forth his hand, in supplication, saying, 'For Mary!' that dead man may have given him silver. Therefore they will cast the soul into the scales, causing it to be weighed, and if Mary but throw her shadow over the soul it will weigh heavy as gold and the pan will descend. So the Devil will depart, releasing the soul, and she will enter it into Gannat, which is Paradise.

But the soul of one who did evil upon earth goes with the Devil, who after chewing it in his mouth takes it to the fire of

Gahannab and there sports with it—at one time steeping it in fire, at another in icy water which shrivels the skin, and at another casting it into darkness. Therefore he who can will give alms to prisoners and to the poor at the enclosure of a church, fearing and honouring the shrine that it may keep him in remembrance. For he will say, 'May the shrine guard my soul that it be healed and be not like to theirs.'

ROYAL CHRONICLES AND HISTORICAL WORKS

The ostensibly secular literature of the fourteenth and fifteenth centuries includes the histories of the Zagwé kings, the dynasty of 'non-Solomonic' and non-Semitic descent who are nevertheless revered in Ethiopia as saintly figures and workers of miracles. The last of these kings abdicated or was deposed about 1270, but these chronicles of their reigns are compositions or revisions of the fifteenth century. They are very largely hagiographical in character, replete with miracles and marvels which are freely interchanged between one Life and another, though the famous Lalibela, creator of rock-churches, attracted the lion's share.

From the fourteenth century onwards many straightforward royal chronicles have been preserved which are the principal source of all subsequent Ethiopian history. Both their historical and literary value are very variable. Many record only the barest and driest outline of events with constant repetition of set literary formulae and excessive use of quotations from scripture. Others, however, especially the 'Chronicle of the Wars of Amda Tsion I' are commended by scholars as lively documents.

One historical treatise, or rather historical romance, translated from the Arabic in the first quarter of the fourteenth century, had extraordinary significance for all the following centuries of Ethiopian history. This was the *Kebra Nagast*, or Glory of Kings, in which, alongside much other material, we find the story of the Queen of Sheba's visit to Solomon, of the birth of Menelik, their son, and of his subsequent visit to Jerusalem, which culminated in his stealing the Ark of the Covenant and carrying it off to Axum. This was not the first appearance in Ethiopia of the Queen of Sheba legend, which must have been current among the Abyssinians for centuries. But the story now had the backing of literary authority and could be clothed in circum‑stantial detail. Henceforth it would be needless to stress the necessity of Solomonic blood in all rulers of Ethiopia. The story related in the *Kebra Nagast* became the national saga of the country, in which every citizen believed implicitly.

POETRY AND SONG

In this field of verse, both secular and religious, scholars have found evidence of much forceful and original expression. Some fourteenth‑century hymns, for instance, present themes of the Passion and stories of the Christian martyrs, often in couplet or dialogue form, which still remain free from the stereotyped conventions which bind later Abyssinian poetry. Of particular interest are some verses on the massacre of the Nadjran Christians in AD 523—an event of historical importance as leading to the Abyssinian conquest of the Yemen. Eight centuries later this tragic but glorious episode still stirred the imagination of the Christian poet.

A more popular and perhaps more spontaneous literary genre, also dating back to the fourteenth century, was the martial chant, or *shillalo*, sung no doubt by soldiers in the field in honour of their leader in battle during the heroic age of Abyssinian history. Evidently such songs were composed, not by professional *literati* but by poets of the people, or by those minstrels who, then as now, accompanied the song on their one‑stringed fiddle or *masinqo*. The language of these chants is not the Ghe'ez which remained obligatory for all recognized literature but a popular speech more like Amharic. The martial chant remained popular for centuries, indeed it has survived until today in the form of the young warriors' war‑songs improvised at *masqal* and other festivals. Notable among early ones that have come down to us is a wonderful panegyric addressed to King Isaac (1414–29), justly singled out by Cerulli (who gives an Italian rendering of it in *Storia della letteratura etiopica*) as a gem of Abyssinian poetry.

Later in the fifteenth century, during the reign of Iskinder or Alexander (1478–94), a new poetic form, the *qené*, makes its first recorded appearance. Many of these poems have a religious character, but, unlike ordinary hymns, the *qené* is a sophisticated form of verse, with severely disciplined metrical structure and highly wrought epigrammatic content. It is deliberately cryptic. Levine (in *Wax and Gold*) says:

> The chief delight of Ethiopic poetry is to attain a maximum of thought with a minimum of words ... the more ingeniously compact and obscure the construction of the verse, the more pleased will be the poet, and his audience.

The *qené*, which may vary in length from two to eleven lines, exists in several recognized varieties. The most interesting of these—but the most difficult to interpret—is the so-called 'wax and gold' or *samenna warq* type. This designation is drawn from the traditional method of casting used by the Abyssinian gold- and silversmiths. Just as precious metal replaces wax in this process of casting, so 'wax and gold' poetry presents two parallel thoughts, or rather one thought embedded in another. One meaning is external and obvious (wax); the other and more important is internal and hidden (gold). This 'dual imagery' is achieved by making the most of the ambiguities of the language, by full use of punning and veiled allusions. Such verses are in their nature incapable of translation. Even in Ethiopia only initiates are expected to appreciate the *qené*, and sometimes no one but the author himself can savour his piece to the full.

Originally these poems were all written in Ghe'ez and reserved for religious use; set to music, they were sung in church at the conclusion of the mass. Later, with increasing popularity, they came to be adapted for various secular purposes: one *qené* might be used for a surreptitious attack on the king which would readily pass from mouth to mouth; another, couched in scriptural phrases, might conceal a love message. In modern times the Amharic language proved to be ideally adapted to this type of esoteric poetry. In fact, it became immensely popular among the Amharas, and remains so today: perhaps it will prove to be the most characteristic expression of their literary genius. There are still schools of *qené* attached to monasteries in the Gojjam and elsewhere.

THE SIXTEENTH CENTURY AND ONWARDS

The basic literature to meet Ethiopia's ecclesiastical needs had all been provided by the end of the fifteenth century. But the fearful crises of the sixteenth century (see Chapter II) brought wholly new circumstances, with the result that a considerable new litera-ture came into being. The old belief that the Moslem wars, closely followed by the invasion of the Gallas, brought a total cessation of all cultural activity is clearly untenable. These events certainly brought widespread devastation and anarchy, impover-ishment, famine and sudden death. Nevertheless, in the midst of these national and personal catastrophes learned hands undertook new translations from Arabic, and even from Latin, and theolo-gians were at work on books in defence of their threatened Christian faith. At the same time the unprecedented events of the day were being carefully recorded, not only by the Abyssinians, whose existence as an independent people was in jeopardy, but also by Moslem chroniclers on the 'enemy' side.

One of the most remarkable characters in Abyssinian literary history was one Salik, an Arab of uncertain origin who settled in Ethiopia under Lebna Denghel—the king who also received the Portuguese embassy in 1520. Salik joined the Christian Church, became a monk under the name of Embakom (Habakkuk) and eventually rose to be abbot of the great monastery of Debra Libanos. This made him *Etcheghé*, i.e. head of all the monasteries—a position no other foreigner has held, before or since. Embakom, who became famous for his learning and religious zeal, was the author of the *Ankasa Amin* (gateway of the Faith) a work of apologetics which, as a convert from Islam, he was peculiarly fitted to write. In it he analyses passages from the Koran to demonstrate Christian truths as he saw them—for instance, the universality of the Gospel compared with the limited appeal of Muhammad. He also defends the Christian conception of the Trinity against the Moslem assertion (then used as anti-Christian propaganda) that it amounted to polytheism; and he offers a thoughtful defence of religious pictures and images, proscribed by Islam. Embakom also translated books from the Arabic including that widespread legend of Indian Buddhist derivation, Baralam and Yewasef.

Among other religious works of the troubled sixteenth century one may mention the *Haymanota Abau* (Faith of the Fathers) containing selections from Athanasius, Cyril, Ambrose and other Fathers of the Church: this superseded the old *qerlos* (St Cyril) and has ever since enjoyed great authority. A book of some historical interest was the *Metsehafa Kedar* (book of impurity) which lays down penances to be performed by apostates returning to the Christian fold. There were many such, for during the Moslem wars apostasy to Islam was often the only alternative to martyrdom open to Abyssinian Christians. A new hagiographical work, the *Acts of St Sebastian*, also came into circulation, and was apparently translated direct from a Latin version. The presence of Roman Catholics was bound to have some influence on the literature, and it was about the middle of the century that King Galawdewos or Claudius, whom the Jesuits had done their best to convert, wrote his well-known 'Confession of Faith', a notable statement of the Ethiopian standpoint on religion.

With regard to the historical records of these tumultuous times, we find that the Abyssinian viewpoint is well represented by a series of royal chronicles, still written in Ethiopic. The Chronicle of Galawdewos (1540–59), Lebna Denghel's son, is an extremely important source for the history of the times, giving the story of the Moslem invasion in some detail. It is interesting that a contemporary Arabic chronicle—the 'History of the Conquests of Abyssinia', written probably by a native of Harar—gives the same story as seen by the Moslem invaders who were still the victors in the conflict. The sufferings of Christian Ethiopia are recorded also, in graphic detail, in a biographical work called the *Acts of Tekla Alfa*—he was the Abbot of a monastery in the Gojjam. Here again there are parallel accounts among the Moslem chronicles showing how tragic was the lot of the ordinary population during these long-continued struggles, whether on one side or the other.

Nor were the troubles of Ethiopia at an end when the Moslem attacks were finally repulsed. The exhaustion and disorganization of the people opened the way for new invaders seeking living-space as much as conquest, and in their greatly superior numbers as formidable as the forces of Grañ. These newcomers were Galla tribes who penetrated the highlands from the south and were to occupy huge tracts of the plateau and the middle levels. This new upheaval again had repercussions in the field of literature. A notable *History of the Gallas* was written in the second half of the sixteenth century by one Bahrey, a priest at the court of Malak Sagad and a writer imbued with the true spirit of historical research.

It is not possible to extend this survey to the seventeenth century, except to mention two works of particular importance. The *Fetha Nagast* (legislation of the kings), a book of legal precepts based on Byzantine law, was translated from the Arabic and it remained immensely influential in Ethiopia until modern times. A compendium of ecclesiastical song, the *deggwa*, also appeared at this time, and is often provided with musical notation in the form of miniature signs and symbols written above the line (see p. 155). The royal chronicles continued to be maintained *Fig. 36* in almost every reign through the seventeenth and eighteenth centuries and on into the nineteenth. While some vernacular words and idioms started creeping in during the eighteenth century, all chronicles were still written in Ethiopic. It was left to the ill-fated emperor Theodore (1855–68) to establish Amharic as the official language for this and other purposes.

Although this section has dealt with books of post-medieval and even modern date, I must conclude with a reminder that they all take the form of manuscripts on parchment. Even though the majority of those now in circulation are of the eighteenth, nineteenth or even twentieth century, they all have an antique aspect and are in fact a remarkable survival of medieval craftsmanship. The work of the best calligraphers can be singularly beautiful, and I was pleased to discover on a recent journey to Ethiopia (1969) that there are still some at work in outlying monasteries.

CHAPTER VI

Painting

L IKE OTHER SCHOOLS of painting, the Abyssinian school is the combined product of foreign and indigenous influences. But in Abyssinia's case the foreign element has been all-powerful. There is little of Africa in their pictorial art. This art remained, until very recent years, purely religious and it derived originally from those countries of the early Christian world which were the source of Ethiopian Christianity itself.

These countries of the eastern Mediterranean and western Asia were geographically remote and the Abyssinians' links with them were tenuous. It is not surprising, therefore, that the models on which their earliest painters depended for inspiration (chiefly, we suppose, illuminated Gospel Books) were few and scarce. But the influence exerted by the few books that did somehow reach the country was, for this reason, all the greater. The isolation of Abyssinia continued, and even as late as the seventeenth century we see the same phenomenon repeated: a single sacred picture striking the local imagination could give rise to a succes-sion of more or less modified derivatives.

Another feature of Abyssinian art, to be illustrated in what follows, was (and is) its persistent adherence to tradition, as a result of which it became a veritable museum of archaic com-positions. However, this conservatism did not prevent a complete departure by local artists from the *style* of the originals. Nor did it prevent a very slow modification of the iconography itself. In the earliest art of the country we see a tendency to simplify traditional compositions and to reduce them to geometrical schemes peopled by rigid, lifeless, frontal figures. Of all Christian schools of art only the Mozarabic, which developed during the Moorish occupation of Spain, presents strikingly similar characteristics— as Sir Wallis Budge pointed out as long ago as 1898.

The conservatism and the continuity displayed by Ethiopian painting, even until modern times, would make it difficult to close this chapter abruptly at the moment when west-European influence began to assume importance early in the seventeenth century. Moreover, to stop at that point would exclude from this survey most of the surviving painting, including much that is peculiarly characteristic of the country. The section of this chapter commencing on p. 147 will therefore deal with later developments in this field.

ILLUMINATED GOSPELS,

FOURTEENTH AND FIFTEENTH CENTURIES

These Gospels are the earliest available source of Abyssinian religious pictures—except possibly for some fragmentary wall paintings. Also, apart from ancient inscriptions, they were the earliest known examples (and very beautiful examples) of Ethiopic calligraphy. However, one manuscript (the Gospels of Abba Garima) recently described, may be as early as the tenth or eleventh century. Though not otherwise illustrated it contains a set of 'Eusebian Canons' in arcaded frames which Leroy has proved to be derived from the early art of Syria as transmitted through later Armenian versions. Since the remark-able sets of pictures which follow the 'Canons' in other early illustrated Gospels had clearly pointed in the same direction, Leroy's conclusion was in no way unexpected, and it accords with the facts of history, for it was Syrian Christianity that first penetrated to Abyssinia. Also, ever since the twelfth century, intermittent contacts had been maintained with that part of the world, and with the kindred Church of Armenia, through the Abyssinian monastic settlement in Jerusalem. One can therefore be sure that some early Gospels, or other books which the Abyssinian artists used as models, were brought from Jerusalem, and some of these were no doubt Armenian.

Plates 29–30

137

Four or five illustrated Gospels of the fourteenth century and about ten of the fifteenth have so far been described, but they continue to come to light. Typically, they open with the letter of Eusebius (3 pages) followed by his 'Canons' or concordance tables of Gospel texts (7 pages), all these ten pages—or at least those of the Canons proper—having arcaded frames. At the end

Plates 76–7 comes a tailpiece of quite a different architectural composition—a gabled *tempietto* with trees and deer commonly called (following Strzygowski) the 'Fountain of Life'. This concluding page of the Canons bears the retrospective inscription: 'Harmony of the four Gospels'.

There follow a series of pictures, which may number up to eighteen, illustrating the life of Christ. They may begin with a few episodes from the life of the Virgin Mary and at least half the series is usually devoted to the Passion. All these pictures come together at the beginning of the book immediately after the Eusebian Canons, but a portrait of each Evangelist makes a frontispiece to his particular Gospel, two of them being sometimes

Plates 74–5 represented standing.

Not only the Canons, but the whole arrangement described including the position and subjects of the pictures, derive from east Christian prototypes. It is most interesting to notice that both Celtic and Carolingian (and pre-Carolingian) illumination was subjected to similar eastern influences: for instance Godescalc's Gospel, commissioned by Charlemagne himself, contains a perfect Fountain of Life, as do subsequent manuscripts associated with the name of his half-sister Ada. So, in this field of early art, the countries of the Far West show a certain kinship with Abyssinia—then the remotest southern outlier of the Christian world.

Figs. 31–2 To illustrate fourteenth-century picture cycles two text-figures are here given after the Lake Hayq Gospels now in Addis Ababa, while eight subjects from the Gospels of Debra Maryam in

Plates 68–75 Eritrea (some as yet unpublished) are reproduced among the

138

Fig. 31   The Nativity and the approach of the Wise Men from a fourteenth-century Gospel-book. The second figure attending on the Virgin is her apocryphal sister, Salome

plates. The old Abyssinian tendency to reduce scenes to a subtle geometry is well shown in the Nativity, the Entombment and the Resurrection. The Arrest of Christ and Peter's Denial are both examples of extreme simplification: the number of figures is reduced to a minimum and the cock has lost his perch. A peculiarly Abyssinian element to be found in these early cycles is the pair of angels whose wings meet to form a canopy overhead, or   *Fig. 32*

139

Fig. 32   The Baptism from the same ms.

Plate 88 the single angel, instrument of God's guidance, as in the Flight into Egypt.

Plate 68 From the point of view of East-Christian iconography there is much of interest here. The remarkable Transfiguration is hardly to be recognized as such, having lost all trace of the Mountain invariably to be seen in the standard Byzantine version of the subject. Does this composition follow some early model Plate 70 now lost or did the Abyssinians invent it? The Crucifixion is equally extraordinary: the middle cross bears no Christ figure, but the Lamb of God floats above it. This composition must go back to the sixth century but no exact parallel is known. Probably both these conceptions were once known in other parts of the Christian East but survive today in Ethiopia alone.

Plate 71 The Entombment, while retaining elements of the normal Byzantine version, is reduced to a geometrical abstraction—powerful, nevertheless, in its impact on the eyes and mind. The Plate 73 Ascension, subject to the stylization inevitable in Abyssinia, has changed little. It was needless, indeed, to alter such an effective rendering of the subject—though it *was* altered (for the worse) in other local versions. It is basically identical to the same subject in the Syriac Gospels of Rabula, of the sixth century—a splendid composition which was repeated much later in Armenian versions.

The most magnificent of all Abyssinian Gospel Books is probably that from the island of Kebran in Lake Tana, dating from the early fifteenth century. As can be seen from its eighteen whole-page pictures (some of which have been beautifully reproduced in the UNESCO art book) this artist's technical skill and his sense of colour show a great advance over anything known from the previous century. At the same time this manuscript belongs to a more conformist school than, for instance, the early Gospels of Lake Hayq and Debra Maryam, and is therefore iconographically less exciting. Its model must have been a comparatively late Gospel or pattern-book embodying the artistic traditions then standardized in the Byzantine world.

BOOK ILLUSTRATIONS, PANELS AND MURAL PAINTINGS, FIFTEENTH AND SIXTEENTH CENTURIES

While illustrated Gospels were still being produced during the fifteenth century, paintings of other subjects and in other media now became important. At least they appear in retrospect to assume importance in these centuries, since so little has survived from any earlier period.

The earlier Gospel-Books reflect Abyssinian dependence upon Syria and Armenia and we might expect to find corresponding evidence of the well-known contacts with Coptic Egypt, on which the Abyssinian Church had to rely for its Abuna. There is indeed evidence of Coptic influence in painting, though exactly how it was transmitted is not so clear, for manuscripts were probably not responsible.

Fig. 33 Double diptych with modern pictures showing, from left to right, an equestrian saint, Galawdewos, St George and the Dragon, and the Trinity. Overall height: 28 cm.

Fig. 33

The equestrian saints so characteristic of Abyssinian painting were almost certainly of Coptic derivation. Figures on horseback were common in late Egyptian and Coptic art. A well-known fifth-century relief (now in the Louvre), which shows a mounted Horus spearing a spirit of evil in the form of a crocodile, suggests a possible origin for St George slaying the dragon and similar subjects, which became widely popular at the time of the Crusades. It was in Egypt too that characteristic colours became associated with the mounts of particular saints: St George's horse is white, St Mercurius's black, St Theodore's red. This tradition was upheld in Abyssinia, where equestrian saints begin

Plate 80

to appear in manuscripts of the fifteenth century and have remained extremely popular ever since.

Another decidedly Coptic motif is the figure with hands upraised in the early Christian attitude of prayer. These *orans* figures are a constant feature of Coptic reliefs in marble and limestone including innumerable funerary stelae, mostly belonging to the fourth and fifth centuries. This subject too spread to Abyssinia, probably in early times. However, the oldest *orantes* we know there appear in fifteenth-century representations of various scriptural (including Old Testament) scenes, such as the three youths in the fiery furnace. Other illustrations of the period contain saints and Fathers of the Church, many of whom adopt the same posture; these pictures are often distinguished by a most remarkable stylization of the features, the hands and the clothes. Also, the Virgin Mary is commonly represented *orans*.

Plates 82–3

Fig. 34

Fig. 34 Detail of a figure of Abba Bisoy, an ascetic of the Egyptian desert, from an early fifteenth-century copy of the Gadla Abau, i.e. Acts of the Fathers (from Playne)

A number of variations on the theme of the Madonna and Child were current in Abyssinia between 1400 and 1600, until all were regrettably superseded by a single standard type early in the seventeenth century. Some of these earlier Madonnas were known to the Copts, who could have passed them on: examples are the Virgin giving suck and the Virgin enthroned with the Child on her lap, both looking directly forward. Whether Coptic Egypt did or did not serve as an intermediary, most Abyssinian Madonnas were certainly derived from East-Christian prototypes, and they often include the characteristic Byzantine throne-cushion. Besides those just mentioned, we find variations of the

Plate 78

late-Byzantine *hodigitria* including that in which the Child embraces his Mother. Another type from the East-Christian world, known from an early wall-painting in a Tigrean rock-church, is the frontal Virgin on whose breast Jesus appears in a circular medallion. Still another is the Madonna as Queen of Heaven, crowned by angels.

In addition to all these there are examples in which the infant

Plate 79

Jesus holds a plaything in the form of a twig or flower, or a bird. These appear to be of West-European origin, which is perfectly feasible since several Italian painters, and one Portuguese, are known to have reached Abyssinia during this period, one of them as early as the beginning of the fifteenth century.

From whatever source these Madonnas were ultimately derived, they soon underwent 'acclimatization' and became distinctively Abyssinian. This was chiefly a stylistic change imposed by the traditions and tastes of the country, or by the capabilities of the artists. But one new feature was introduced to modify the icono-graphy itself: almost every Abyssinian Madonna is flanked by the Archangels Michael and Gabriel with swords drawn and raised to protect her.

Most of the attractive Madonna-types described above are to be found painted (usually in tempera) on the wooden panels which, as diptychs, double diptychs, and triptychs, are still to be found in the treasuries of some Abyssinian churches. Many beautiful ones, some dating from the period now being considered, have been collected in the Museum of the Institute of Ethiopian Studies at the University of Addis Ababa. In these examples the Virgin and Child very often figure on the left wing of a diptych or the central panel of a triptych. Other subjects frequently represented are the Crucifixion, the Twelve Apostles together with St Paul, numerous cavalier saints on horses of various colours and the Trinity represented as three identical old men. (This curious subject, proscribed in the West at the Council of Trent but still popular in Ethiopia, was also known in the Nile Valley, for it occurs among frescoes of the twelfth century from the Christian site of Faras.)

Fig. 33

These paintings are in general extremely naive and, by most outside standards, absurdly incompetent in execution. The drawing is linear and flat with no attempt to give the illusion of volume or perspective. The colour range is strictly limited and subtle tones are seldom achieved. Figures have little recognizable anatomy and their proportions are freely varied to fit the available space. Yet the marvel is that this most isolated outpost of Christen⁄dom should have any Christian art in the generally understood sense at all. Seen from this point of view the interest of these paintings is very great. Moreover they reflect a deep and un⁄questioning faith and, for those accustomed to local modes of expression, sometimes have a haunting beauty.

Isolated wall⁄paintings of the fifteenth and sixteenth centuries are still numerous in the older Abyssinian churches, including many rock⁄hewn ones, but the people never valued early work for its own sake and the vast majority have been obliterated. Never⁄theless we already know of two rock⁄hewn churches which retain complete schemes of mural decoration dating apparently from before the massive impact of external influences that occurred in the seventeenth century. Of slight interest architecturally, both ramify in the rock but are hardly visible outside. One, Yadibba

Plates 84–5   Maryam in Daunt, is reached by a mule journey of five days north-westwards from Dessie and has very rarely been seen by outsiders. The other is the church of Abba Yemata near Guh in Gheralta, north of Makalle; to visit it one must face a distinctly alarming climb up one of the castellated sandstone crags which abound in this district.

The decoration of Yadibba Maryam was planned as a whole and the 'frescoes' are of a scale to suit the dimensions of the church itself. The walls are divided (though not rigidly) into upper and lower registers, the lower being largely peopled by equestrian figures, the upper by rows of saints and patriarchs including David with harp, and Solomon with sword. (Many of these figures are full-face, but others are shown three-quarter face, which is something of a novelty. Profiles are reserved for evil

Fig. 35   people.) We also find the Cappadocian martyr Mamas riding upon a rather comical lion (the legend tells that he was thrown to the lions under Aurelian, but ended up astride one of them). At the top of the walls are bands of interlaced ornament. In the sanctuaries of the church (four in number) these bands are surmounted by the most effective decoration of all, for the domed ceilings are adorned with circles of sword-bearing angels. In the sanctuary of St George (now again in use and so unfortunately inaccessible) these are in turn surrounded by four additional angels with outspread, interlocking wings.

At Guh a comparable scheme in a very similar style is developed; the condition of the frescoes is even more perfect, their colours deeper and more varied. The two domes attract particular attention. Both are ringed round with a broad band of geometrical ornament within which a number of half-figures are ranged in a circle, their haloed or turbaned heads in the centre, books or crosses in their hands. One of these dome-paintings represents nine of the Apostles, the other, eight of the 'Nine Saints', the semi-legendary founders of Abyssinian monasticism. The abandoned chapel of Abba Daniel at Qorqor, not far from Guh,

Fig. 35 Wall painting of St Mamas on lion-back from Yadibba Maryam. Sixteenth century ?

also has a singularly effective (and possibly contemporary) design in its rock-hewn dome. There are four saintly figures, between whom stand four angels with outspread wings, and the angels' wing-tips touch the wing-tips of the adjoining angels over the heads of the saints. Gerster's book, *Churches in Rock,* contains fine photographs both of Guh and Qorqor.

These sets of wall-paintings are conspicuously lacking in many subjects which became popular (indeed universal) from the seventeenth century onwards. It therefore seems highly probable that the schemes described were carried out by artists unaware of these new trends some time before the end of the sixteenth century.

LATER PHASES OF PICTORIAL ART, SEVENTEENTH CENTURY AND AFTER

The overwhelming majority of extant Ethiopian paintings, whether they adorn the pages of manuscripts, the walls of churches, or the panels of diptychs and triptychs, are no earlier than the seventeenth and eighteenth centuries. During those two hundred years the kings ruled from Gondar and an important school of art flourished there under royal patronage. The character of this art is still unmistakably Abyssinian even though marked new elements, both of style and subject matter, now appear. It is a mistake to describe these later pictures as 'Portuguese'. Whatever new subjects came in from Europe they were never distinctively Portuguese, and in any case their style was wholly transmuted in accordance with local taste. The traditions established at this period have remained in force until the present day.

It was in the seventeenth century, above all, that some entirely new subjects were introduced, and these were soon added to the local artists' stock-in-trade. During the influential years of the Jesuit Mission various books, pictures and prints which presented scriptural subjects in a manner quite new to the Abyssinians were brought in by the missionaries. Even when the Roman Catholic doctrine was rejected and systematically rooted out, and the Mission forcibly and violently disbanded, some pictorial themes they had introduced enjoyed an extraordinary success, flowering, as Monneret expressed it, after the parent plant had died. We must mention several well documented instances.

Monneret de Villard proved that the type of Virgin and Child almost universally accepted in Abyssinia after the beginning of the seventeenth century is based on the famous Madonna 'of St Luke' in Santa Maria Maggiore in Rome. This picture is an Italo-Byzantine *hodigitria* of the thirteenth century in which the Child is carried on the Virgin's *left* arm (unlike most Madonna-types previously known in Abyssinia). Abyssinian versions of this portrait of the Virgin, though they fail to convey her spiritu-ality, repeat every detail of her own and the Child's posture, the position of the hands being especially characteristic. This picture probably became widely known through engravings circulated by the Jesuits. It seems, however, that there were also later types of Italian Madonna in circulation at the time, or that these prints showed adjuncts which the original does not possess. For many of the seventeenth-century Abyssinian versions have angels holding a drapery behind the Virgin, their hands grasping the looped edges of the cloth, exactly as in some of Duccio's fourteenth-century Madonnas.

A similar story has been worked out by Cerulli in relation to the 'Ecce Homo' or Christ with Crown of Thorns. A version of this subject became widespread in Abyssinia in the seventeenth century and appears again and again in various media. The *Fig. 48* subject was traced to a single picture, of late-Gothic origin but painted by a Portuguese artist under Flemish influence, and this reached Gondar in the seventeenth century. (The painting in question, taken by the Napier Expedition from Magdala in 1868, is now in England.)

More recently, Leroy (following up a suggestion of Buchthal's) has shown that a whole family of Gospel-illustrations, produced in Gondar later in the same century, were copied from Germanic prints in the tradition of Dürer. These subjects, re-engraved by Tempesta, were used to illustrate the Arabic Gospels published in Rome in 1591. It was this Gospel-Book that reached Gondar and from which a number of biblical subjects were copied by the local artists, who kept to the original compositions but radically changed their style.

These examples show that, even as late as the seventeenth century, Abyssinia was starved of artistic models and ready to seize upon new ideas (if they happened to appeal to local taste) with enthusiasm. In spite of transforming the originals stylistically (no doubt a subconscious process) artists still treated their models with apparently needless deference and dared not tamper with their main lines. This is why anything like local colour is so disappointingly scarce in Abyssinian illumination. In the eighteenth century more liberties were taken and some pictures do, at last, illustrate the life of the country: see for instance two versions of the Flight into Egypt included in the plates. *Plates 89, 90*

The paintings of the Gondar school, whatever their medium or their setting, can be distinguished at a glance from those of earlier centuries. Contacts with the outside world have resulted in a far wider range of subjects, in a greater variety of expressions, attitudes and groupings, in a new flexibility of line and less restricted use of colour. It is also possible to distinguish an earlier and a later Gondar 'manner'. The first is still mainly an art of outline-drawing. In the second, figures are shown to some extent 'in the round' while pictures are often provided with decorative borders, and given backgrounds of vivid colour. These various advances certainly produced a colourful and popular style of painting, even though most devotees of Ethiopian art infinitely prefer the rigid but powerful productions of earlier times.

While most of these later paintings show direct influence from the West, others seem to betray an indirect effect of the European presence in Ethiopia. The Jesuits were based on Goa, the Indian port from which the early Portuguese navigators had explored the Red Sea region. It seems possible that, through Goa, the folk art (or the *Catholic* folk art) of India could have influenced some Ethiopian scriptoria. Monneret de Villard first suggested this to account for the series of pictures illustrating some late copies of the

Plates 91–2 *Miracles of the Virgin Mary* (e.g. the Lady Meux MS. edited by Budge). The *Miracles* are part of Abyssinian folklore and, since they had never before been illustrated, these pictures are of particular interest. They have a 'narrative' style, several scenes being combined, without any particular order, in a single plate, while some common postures are thought to be of Asiatic origin.

Although new departures like these did characterize manuscript art of the seventeenth and eighteenth centuries, it must not be forgotten that traditional forces were still alive, if less powerful than hitherto. Indeed, some late manuscripts still contain illustrations of incredibly archaic character. A notable example is Oriental 481 in the British Museum, a large, almost square volume of the Octateuch, Gospels and *Senodos*, written in the late seventeenth century. Here we find, for instance, a Transfiguration and an Ascension of purely Byzantine type (taken, of course, from local Gospels illuminated two or three hundred years before) while *two* Crucifixions are included, one of traditional Eastern and one of intrusive Western character. Interesting examples of archaic stylization occur in other coeval manuscripts, and in the folded parchment strips found by Beatrice Playne in Lasta.

Plate 81

Turning to the pictorial decoration of churches, we find the same Gondar style familiar from manuscripts, but a few complete schemes exist which throw light on the general programme the artists had in mind. A recent study by Staude deals with two such schemes. One belonged to the church of Abba Antonios near Gondar: the original paintings were removed to Paris in 1933 by Marcel Griaule and are now on view at the Musée de l'Homme. The other set is still to be seen in the charming church of Debra Sina on the shore of Lake Tana near Gorgora—a round church with steep, conical thatched roof. In both instances a square sanctuary rises within the circular outer wall, and the outside of the sanctuary is entirely covered with pictures painted on cloth glued to the walls. Another church just outside Gondar—Debra Berhan Selassie—is often visited for the sake of its attractive but much restored mural paintings of the same period (late seventeenth to early eighteenth century). Here, however, they are of necessity arranged in a different way: the nave (like the whole church) is rectangular and its four *inside* walls are covered with pictures from top to bottom. It also has a most decorative ceiling with numerous winged heads of cherubs—an idea derived, of course, from Western Europe.

cf. Plate 86

To see the painted walls of a Debra-Sina-type church one must pass round the ambulatory which encircles the Holy of Holies in a clockwise direction, beginning with the eastern wall. A typical theme here is the prelude to the coming of Christ. The pictures portray patriarchs and prophets and those events of the Old Testament which foreshadow events of the New. There is

Abraham's sacrifice of Isaac, anticipating Christ's sacrifice. There is Daniel among the lions, and Jonah with the whale—both incidents which were taken to symbolize Christ's resurrection after three days. The adjoining south wall shows the Visitation, the Nativity, the Massacre of the Innocents and Flight into Egypt—i.e. the First Coming of Christ. Alongside these scenes the Second Coming is shown as well—a Last Judgment surmounting a fiery scene of the Devil chained in hell. This wall also carries the Apostles (with St Paul) and the Nine Saints who were in a sense the Apostles of Ethiopia.

The west wall is the most important of all since it faces the main door of the church, and here some basic doctrines are illustrated. Over the entrance to the sanctuary is Christ crowning the Virgin Mary in heaven—a scene intended to represent the Covenant of Mercy—with God the Father above. The Madonna and Child and the Crucifixion balance each other to right and left of the sanctuary door, as in many diptychs. Nearer ground level we find local saints—Tekla Haymanot, Abuna Gabra Manfas Qiddus and others. Also St George, king of saints and such a well-loved patron that he too is given a place of special honour. Further round to the left, the north wall is devoted in large part to those who were martyred for the faith including Stephen the Protomartyr, St Peter and St Paul. There is also a decorative row of warrior saints riding horses of different colours and spearing various animal or half-human forms, each the embodiment of some sin or evil.

Plate 87

These fine picture-cycles, compared by Staude to 'a symphony in four movements', were intended both to adorn and to instruct: without doubt they were well fitted to do both. They represent the art of Gondar at its best. In the hands of itinerant painters the art of this school has since spread all over the country, producing many attractive pictures if few masterpieces.

Since the latter part of the nineteenth century Ethiopian painter-craftsmen have turned out pictures, on parchment or on cloth, for the private buyer. They include non-religious subjects such as battle-scenes, courts of law, feasts and festivals; also the ever-popular legend of Solomon and the Queen of Sheba in 'strip cartoons' of twenty-four to ninety-six scenes. Though hardly to be classed as art, they sometimes have historic or sociological interest and they are undoubtedly effective as decoration. Also, such is the strength of tradition in that ancient land, that even the crudest of these pictures, hawked in the streets of Addis Ababa or Asmara, seem to preserve a little of the character of old Ethiopia.

CHAPTER VII

The Other Arts

MUSIC AND MUSICAL INSTRUMENTS

THE ABYSSINIANS attribute the invention of their ecclesiastical music—with its rhythms, its modes, its notation, its
accompanying dance—to Yared, a sixth-century saint of treas-
ured memory. Among other episodes of Yared's life, the *Synaxarium* gives the following:

> One day whilst St Yared was singing by the foot-stool of King
> Gabra Masqal the king was so deeply absorbed in listening
> to his voice, that he drove his spear into Yared's foot with such
> force that much blood spurted out; but St Yared did not know
> of it until he had finished his song. And when the king saw
> this he was dismayed, and he drew his spear out of his foot,
> and said to him: 'Ask me whatever reward you wish in return
> for your blood which has been shed'; and St Yared said to
> him . . . 'send me away that I may become a monk'.

The *Acts* of Yared, composed by a priest of Axum or Debra
Damo, probably in the late fifteenth century, contain the following passage—another reminder of the all-absorbing appeal of the
sacred song and dance:

> When the priests and deacons sing as they have learnt from
> Yared they do it to the point of complete exhaustion, until
> sweat bursts from their pores, until their limbs are out of con-
> trol . . . until their throats are hoarse, until their knees tremble
> and their hands, with which they clap while they sing, are raw.

The *Acts* conclude with the 'effigies' of Yared—probably a later
addition—a poem in which every part of his body is celebrated
in no fewer than forty-eight verses.

The largely vocal music of the Abyssinians—both religious and secular—is replete with tuneful passages which, however, the western ear grasps with difficulty as they do not fit the eight-tone scale. Some of this music is said to be pentatonic, but further study will probably complicate rather than simplify the picture. Abyssinian music has little or nothing in common with that of Africa; its roots (as in other fields of art) are in the East-Christian world and may indeed go further back, like the chant it accompanies, to Hebraic sources.

Most of the liturgy, besides the Psalms and the hymns of the *deggwa* and other collections, are chanted in church and many copies of those books contain a form of notation to remind the singers of the music to which each piece should be sung. In spite of the popular attribution of the system to Yared, it is perhaps more realistic to believe that it was introduced, or assumed its present form, in the sixteenth century, as recorded in the chronicle of King Claudius (1540–59). This notation, written-in above the lines of text, consists in part of Ethiopic letters and in part of other marks or signs. The letters are abbreviations of key words from the liturgy, or from well-known lines in the *deggwa*, the

Fig. 36

Fig. 36   Example of Ethiopian musical notation from a breviary

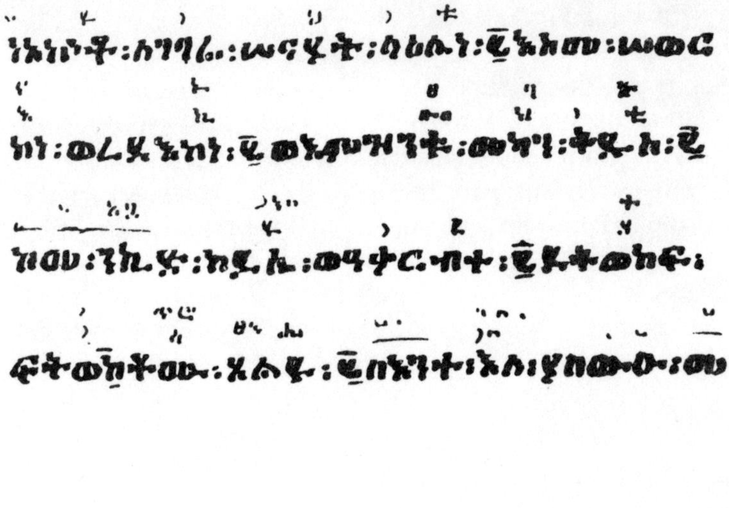

Praises of the Virgin, etc., used as transposable symbols for the melodies to which these words or passages are traditionally sung. The other marks or signs assist the singer to interpret the melody correctly, e.g. they may indicate a pause, a drop in the voice, or words to be sung *staccato, accelerando* or *glissando*. Although comparisons may be made with the 'ecphonetic' notation of Byzantium, and of derivative systems formerly used by the Copts and Armenians, the Abyssinian notation seems to be the only one of its kind still in use today.

Another factor must also be considered, for two rows of musical symbols are sometimes written in over the same lines of text. This indicates that the passage in question should be sung, according to season and circumstances, in one of two alternative 'modes' (which Powne in his *Ethiopian Music* says should rather be called 'moods'). There are three possible modes (reputedly devised by Yared himself) of which the simplest and probably the oldest is called *ghe'ez*—the name also applied to the ancient language of the country. This mode is said to be appropriate for week-days and ordinary occasions. The mode known as *ezel*, low-voiced, slow and dignified, is for fasts, vigils and funerals. On the other hand *araray* (which may be written in red symbols) is light and gay, has higher notes and other embellishments, and is reserved for great festivals.

Plate 12
Fig. 37

Of musical instruments, two only are confined to church use: these are the long double-ended drum, *kabaro*, and the *tsenatsil* or sistrum, both indispensable to the performance of the liturgical dances. Both have been thought to derive from Egypt, though a comparison of the Ethiopian and ancient Egyptian sistra shows considerable differences. There is another drum, hemispherical in shape and provided with one ox-hide tympanum only, which is struck with bent sticks, not with the hand. This is the *negarit*, formerly the attribute of authority—especially the imperial authority. Proclamations read in the market used to be preceded by the beating of this drum, and the Ethiopian Government's official gazette is called the *Negarit Gazeta*. In former times *negarits* were carried in pairs on muleback, their total number varying according to the rank of the dignitary in whose train they were travelling, and they were beaten to announce his coming.

Several wind instruments are (or were) also devoted to cere-monial use. Such are the *imbilta*, a big, primitive flute producing one note only, and the *malakat* or trumpet, with either of which, or both together, fanfares could be blown to herald the approach of important personages. The smaller and more effective type of flute, the *washint*, has four finger-holes and so can yield five notes (or ten with the aid of over-blowing). This is still in use for music-making.

Still more interesting and characteristic of the country are the stringed instruments, especially perhaps the one-stringed *masinqo*. This curious type of fiddle is related to the Arabian *rebab* and to other ancient instruments as far afield as Asia Minor and even Europe. The square or diamond-shaped wooden sound-box, set diagonally, is left open above and below until wrapped round and closed with cowhide, which is stitched up along the sides. The string consists of several strands of horsehair, as does the string of the bow. The musicians' skilful fingering and bowing draw a wider range of notes from the single string than might be thought possible. (Fig. 38.)

The *masinqo* is associated more particularly with the *azmari* or wandering poet-minstrel, the nearest approach in the modern world to the troubadours and minnesingers of the Middle Ages. Though not often seen today, these *azmaris* played no small part in Abyssinian life until very recent times, for they were attached to the households of great men, were regular visitors to markets and drinking-houses, and appeared without fail at all public and private festivities. They sang songs of love and war and traditional ballads in which their audience eagerly joined. They were famous, too, for but slightly veiled comment on potentates and personages of the day. Their pointed wit and skill in ambiguity, often risqué

Fig. 37   The Abyssinian liturgical sistrum or rattle, compared with the early Egyptian prototype above it, from a statue of the cat-headed goddess Bast

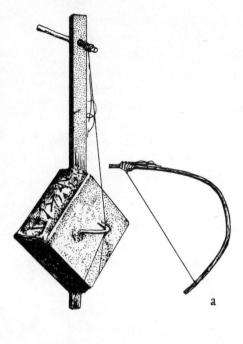

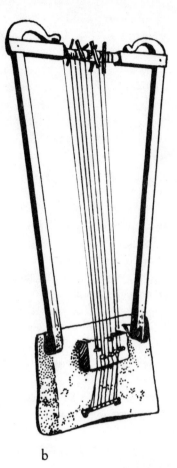

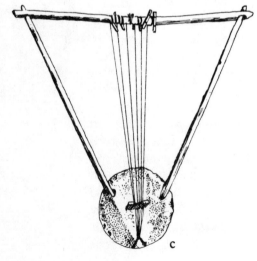

Fig. 38   Stringed instruments: a, masinqo; b, begena; c, krar

or downright outrageous, endeared them to an audience with few outlets for their secret feelings, for nobody was too highly placed to suffer scorn or ridicule at the minstrel's hands. They have mostly vanished, but their memory remains.

Two other stringed instruments, both normally played with a plectrum, are the *begena* and the *krar*, the lyres of Ethiopia. The former is regarded as the more honourable instrument and high-born youths might learn to play it. It is comparatively large, carefully made, and is stood on the ground for playing. Its eight or ten strings give it a good range of notes but it is normally used for serious music only—for accompanying, for instance, the more reputable secular songs as well as religious ones. On the other hand the six-stringed *krar*, of typical triangular form, is a popular instrument carried on the arm and used for lighter music. It is often cheaply made with no better sounding-box, nowadays, than an enamel plate. In spite of their different shapes these are closely related instruments whose resemblance to the lyres of the old Egyptians, Hebrews and Greeks is obvious. The Ethiopians' firm belief that the *begena* is descended from the 'harp' of David may not be without foundation.

Fig. 38 b, c

CARVING IN STONE AND WOOD

The art of figure-sculpture, well known to pre-Axumite civiliza-tion, afterwards died out. The Axumites lost interest in this art-form or, more probably, were influenced by the biblical injunction against 'graven images'. On the other hand use must always have been made of decorative wood-carving at least in conjunction with architecture, but the superb carved ceiling at Debra Damo is the only relic of its kind. Its animal motifs appear to be of pre-Christian and probably west-Asian origin: I do not believe they are based upon the local fauna.

Plate 104

In medieval times stone-sculpture took the form of hewing whole churches from the rock, but there was also some renewed interest in decorative carving as an adjunct to architecture. I have

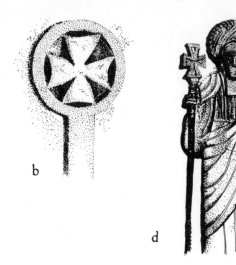

Fig. 39 Comparison of Coptic (left) and Abyssinian (above) stone carving. a, from tombstone of Apa Dorotheus, British Museum; b, pilaster-cross from the rock-hewn church of Cherqos Wuqro; c, from a tombstone in the Coptic Museum, Cairo; d, relief from the Golgotha chapel, Lalibela

Fig. 39

Pates, 57
97–8

already referred to the tall mural reliefs of saints at Lalibela (p. 110). There are also examples among the rock-hewn churches of carved crosses, usually adorning a pillar or pilaster. It is significant that in both cases Coptic Egypt provides very close parallels. Though the Coptic examples belong to a much earlier period, it is hardly possible to question the link. The elaborate geometrical carving applied to panels and arches in churches, originally in wood but copied later in the rock-churches, has also been mentioned. Here again Coptic art provides prototypes, and one may well believe that immigrant Coptic craftsmen were the carriers of this influence, which afterwards became an established tradition in the hands of local wood-carvers.

Some church fittings carry on the same tradition, for they are adorned with similar or even identical carved woodwork. The *manbara tabot* of old Abyssinian churches—a stand for the *tabot* roughly corresponding to an altar—may have decorative panels of this sort, which have sometimes survived when the *manbar* itself has disappeared. Also, portable *manbars* exist which may be beautifully carved with geometrical motifs, very occasionally with figures. They contain a cavity, closed by a hinged door, in which one or two *tabots* of small size could have stood. One of those illustrated is an exceptionally small one, carved from one piece of wood and bearing plain crosses only; it is now in the Ash-molean Museum, Oxford. These portable altars were used when churches had to be mobile, as when emperors were moving from camp to camp or marching to war. (Small chests of this form may have been known in Egypt, for the British Museum possesses a 'stibium caddy' which seems to be a miniature replica of one.)

Fig. 40

Plates 99, 102–3

Fig. 40 Wooden portable altars at Lalibela: the usual type and, right, the eight-legged, cruciform type. Height: c. 50 cm. (from Bidder)

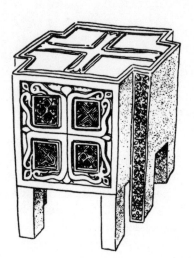

The *tabot* itself is the consecrated slab (representing the Ark of the Covenant or the tablets of the Law contained therein) which converts a mere building into a church, and which is desecrated if seen by any layman's eye. These square or oblong slabs may be of stone but are more usually wooden. They vary in length from a maximum of some 40 cm. down to as few as 15 cm., the shorter ones being thicker, so that they can stand upright like a book. They often bear some carved geometrical decoration and one or more incised crosses. A short incised inscription indicates the dedication, which in both *tabots* illustrated is to *Kidané Meheret*— the Covenant of Mercy.

Plates 100–1

Many processional and manual crosses are made of wood and some of them are very beautifully carved. Brief reference to these is made in the sections on crosses below.

METALWORK

The metalworkers even of pre-Axumite times displayed great skill in their craft. They produced a wide range of bronze vessels, lamps, weapons and tools, and the attractive but mysterious 'identity marks' referred to on p. 36, also some articles of iron. Gold was employed by the Axumites for jewellery though the principal gold hoard unearthed in recent years (at Matara) consisted of imported Roman and Byzantine objects. Gold coins were minted by most Axumite kings between the third and eighth centuries AD, though the majority of their coins were bronze, and a few silver. All these objects throw light on the early civilizations of the country, but it would be impossible to include a description of them in this book. The same applies to domestic wares like pottery and glass. All I can attempt here is to describe some typical products of the metalworker's ancient craft which have lived on into the modern world.

In the field of ecclesiastical metalwork one thinks above all of the crosses, which are considered in their own sections below. There are also characteristic and beautiful bronze censers with

Plate 96

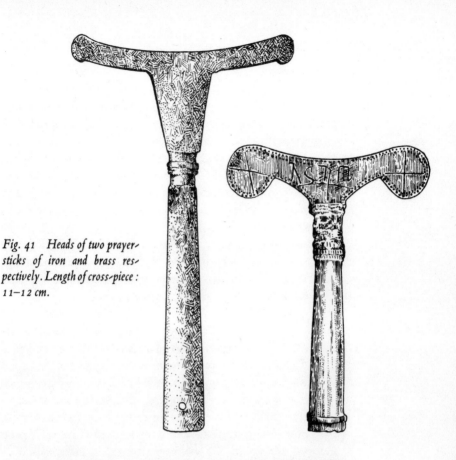

Fig. 41 Heads of two prayer-sticks of iron and brass respectively. Length of cross-piece: 11–12 cm.

round or rectangular incense-bowl and open-work foot and lid; the latter is ringed so that, when raised, it slides up the four chains by which the whole is suspended and swung. Two crutch-shaped heads of 'prayer-sticks' (*maqwamiya*) are illustrated here; others have spherical tops. In poor country churches and remote monasteries, however, one only sees wooden ones cut from local trees, often weirdly bent and twisted but all terminating in a T-shape at the top.

Royal crowns are considered sacred objects, to be stored in church treasuries. A number of these are preserved in the cathedral of St Mary of Zion at Axum, and single ones in many other

Fig. 41

churches. I am not aware of any really early Abyssinian crowns: those mentioned date from the late seventeenth century onwards and have the intricacy to be expected in relatively modern objects intended for royal use. Something very like the pierced metalwork of certain crowns is also seen in a small brass lectern from Eritrea.

Plates 127–8

The other objects shown are in silver more or less adulterated (like the majority of 'silver' crosses) with base metals. Silver was never common in Abyssinia in early times and was still scarce when the kings ruled from Gondar in the seventeenth and eighteenth centuries. Since then the main source of silver has been the Maria Theresa dollar, always dated 1780, which began to reach the towns of Tigrai via Red Sea ports some years after that date. (This handsome coin remained in universal use in Ethiopia until it ceased to be legal tender in the mid-1940s.)

Along with the material the *cire perdue* technique was revived or re-introduced. Many crosses are still made in this way. So are more complicated objects such as silver *birelés* with their spherical body and long, narrow neck, which have to be cast round a solid core. These vessels are shaped like their glass counterparts which are invariably used for drinking *tej*, the Abyssinian mead or honey-wine. In one of the plates an example of such a vessel is shown, as well as a drinking-cup of more normal shape. This is a glorified replica of the ordinary country tumbler made of earthenware or horn and used for water, milk or *talla*, the local beer. The other silver objects shown together with these are a personal seal and several ornaments for women's necklaces, including the ear-picks whose handles are often the object of carefully studied decoration.

Plates 93–5

PENDANT OR PECTORAL CROSSES

These small crosses, worn by every Ethiopian Christian, exist in endless variety and, like other local types of cross, could be made the subject of rewarding studies. Probably such crosses—which would then have been made of bronze—were worn in the early

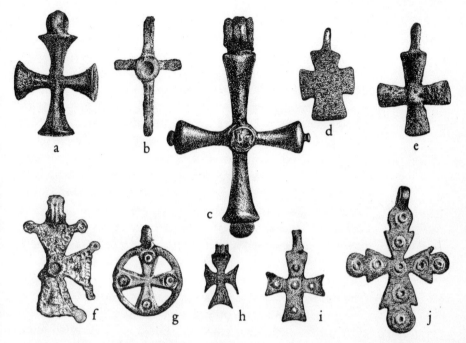

Fig. 42   Coptic pendant crosses of uncertain age and provenance from the collection of the British Museum (a–c, f, h–j) and the Ashmolean, Oxford (d, e, g). Slightly reduced

centuries of Abyssinian Christianity. Afterwards they seem to have gone out of use until Zar'a Yaqob insisted on a revival of the custom in the fifteenth century. In any case, it is hardly possible for *silver* crosses to be older than the early nineteenth century when the metal first became generally available, and those who collect pectoral crosses today find no really ancient examples. Nevertheless they are things of great intrinsic beauty and their designs encourage fascinating trains of thought.

One of the most popular types still worn in Ethiopia is the cross *pattée* with or without a trefoil or other projection at the ends of the arms (a in the accompanying figure). This cross takes one right

Fig. 43

Fig. 42

back to the catacombs where similar ones were painted, or incised on marble slabs. A comparison with Coptic crosses collected in Upper and Lower Egypt is even more instructive: these have the same ring for suspension and a number of virtually identical shapes, so that they could circulate today in Ethiopia without attracting special attention.

Fig. 43

It was customary to wear the smallest of these crosses on the short neck-cord and some of these are particularly attractive owing to their three-dimensional form (b and c); the larger ones would usually be worn on a longer cord or necklace, especially by women. Though hinged crosses were not unknown to the Byzantines the hinge, in Ethiopia, seems to be an indication of very recent date. Evidence for this is to be found in the piece above the hinge which is often crown-shaped or derived by easy stages from the crown. Both hinge and crown show that the insignia of European civil and military orders have influenced Abyssinian cross-design in the last hundred years.

Plate 105

In the plate devoted to pectoral crosses, forms derived from the croix pattée (expanding arms) are shown in the top two rows, those with parallel-sided arms in the third and fourth; the crosses in the bottom row are miscellaneous. In both main categories there are some examples in which the lower limb of the cross is elongated as in the 'Latin' cross, though the majority are 'Greek', or equal-armed. An additional element in some crosses of both categories is an inscribed square (giving points between the arms) or a superimposed ring. It is noticeable that although strictly parallel-sided arms were not popular, crosses of this type were the starting-point for two important sub-categories: the trefoiled crosses, and those with complicated open-work patterns.

Fig. 43

It is not difficult to follow the development of simpler into more complex cross-forms, two such series being shown on the opposite page. The series d–f speaks for itself. In the case of g–i, we begin with a simple two-strand twist or interlacement like those found in reliefs of the eighth and ninth centuries in northern

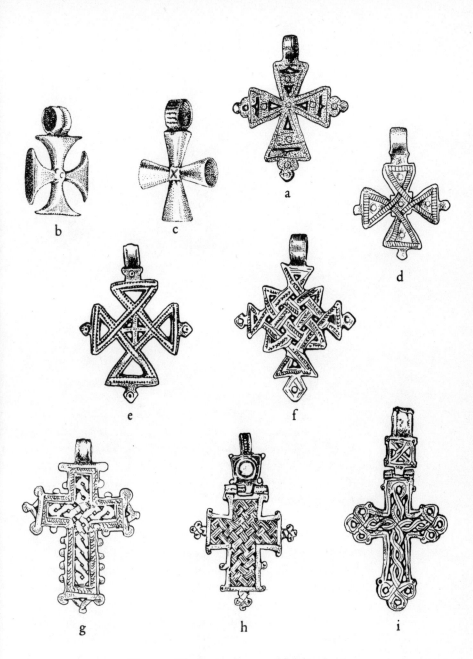

Fig. 43   Silver pectoral crosses. Slightly reduced

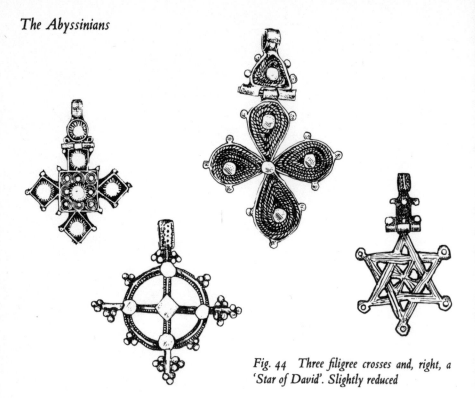

Fig. 44   *Three filigree crosses and, right, a 'Star of David'. Slightly reduced*

Italy and elsewhere, and attributed to Lombard influence. This attractive design penetrated the Byzantine world and somehow travelled on to Ethiopia. The three-stranded plait is an elaboration on the same theme while the third example shown is an elegant modern derivative.

All the crosses so far mentioned are cast or cut in one piece; a few are filed out from whole, unmelted Maria Theresa dollars. *Fig. 44* However, there are filigree crosses as well, in which silver wire and small pellets are soldered on to build up the design; some popular types are here illustrated. A few of the pendants worn as crosses are hardly recognizable as such. Among these is the so-called 'Star of David' and it is interesting that a Judaic symbol should, in this context, be given equal rights with the cross.

PRIESTS' MANUAL CROSSES

If the pectoral crosses are an inheritance from early Christian
times, this is not true of the priests' crosses which, in Abyssinia,
assumed a form quite unknown elsewhere in the Christian world. Plates 106–16
At the lower end of the stem (by which the cross is held) there is a
rectangular base thought to represent the *tabot* of the churches.
Every priest carries one of these crosses which he will produce
whenever necessary, and passers-by will first touch the cross with
their forehead, then kiss it.

*Fig. 45 Priests' crosses from early mss. The figures holding the crosses are, from left to right:
St Timothy (fifteenth-century ms. of the Epistles, now in Addis Ababa); the Archangel Gabriel
from an Annunciation (fifteenth-century Gospels of Yehyeh Ghiorghis); St Cyriacus (early
sixteenth-century Gospels of Betalehem); a saint from a fifteenth-century ms. at Gunda Gunde*

Fig. 46   Priests' crosses of iron and brass. Length : 20–25 cm.

The Other Arts

One would wish to know when this unusual type of cross first came into use. It cannot have been later than the fifteenth century, since they are occasionally introduced into scriptural scenes in illustrated manuscripts of the period. However it is clear that at that time the Abyssinians had not finally opted for the type of priest's cross universal today. Small, plain crosses on long staves (such as are still sometimes carried by monks and nuns) seem to have been an alternative type, while an intermediate form, having an expanded base combined with an extremely long stem, can also be found in miniatures.

Fig. 45

These crosses may be made in any metal or in wood. Those made of softer metals (especially silver and its various alloys) naturally tend to be the most complicated in design. Since they have to be laboriously filed out, iron crosses usually have the simplest, but also very satisfying shapes as can be seen from the figure on the opposite page. Both the brass cross which accom-panies it and one of the iron crosses shown in plate 107 represent a common and popular type. This is a late design associated more particularly with Gondar, but the idea that the Portuguese introduced it (as some writers have thought) is in my opinion without foundation.

Fig. 46

It is noteworthy that few designs are shared between the three main classes of Ethiopian cross. The shape of only one of the pectoral crosses illustrated (i.e. the common Gondarine type just mentioned) is familiar among priests' crosses, and few of the latter can be closely paralleled among processional crosses. Nevertheless these two last-mentioned groups do hold one feature in common which is peculiarly Ethiopian: their heads tend to lose the form of the traditional cross and approximate more and more closely to a diamond shape.

Brass and silver priests' crosses (unlike the plainer iron ones) often have such elaborate open-work designs that the basic cross-motif almost disappears from view. The projecting trefoils in which the arms of the cross terminate develop into clusters of subsidiary crosses while other, diagonal, motifs fill the spaces between the arms. Sometimes little birds adorn the margins of the cross, possibly as symbols of the Holy Spirit. They could have been suggested by the birds which are often scattered round the ornamental frames of canon-tables in early Abyssinian Gospels.

Plates 113–16   Wooden crosses, as might be expected, attract a different type of decoration: they are seldom elaborately pierced but offer ample spaces for superficial carving, often carried out with great care and delicacy. They seem to have been a speciality of the Gondar region (Beghemdir) and the adjoining province of Gojjam, whence today they stream into the market of Addis Ababa for the benefit of foreign collectors. Some church treasuries contain comparatively enormous crosses of this type. These would not be carried by priests for everyday purposes but are reserved (like real processional crosses) for use in procession on special occasions.

PROCESSIONAL CROSSES

The great majority of the processional crosses in use today are of the over-all form described above as distinctively Abyssinian. That is, they have departed widely from the ordinary cross-shape by the elaboration of the whole design and by its tendency to spread into, and even completely fill in, the angles between the arms. This gives them the general shape of a tilted square or diamond. Also, they are provided with metal loops at their base from which the coloured cloths are hung which swathe the crosses when not in use. These various features attract the eye without fail when an Abyssinian processional cross is seen in some unaccustomed setting, such as a Western church or museum.

Plates 123–7   These unmistakable crosses are clearly the end-product of an evolutionary process which must have lasted for hundreds of years and was still continuing in the seventeenth and eighteenth centuries. It is not so easy to say when the process began or how it proceeded and the illuminated manuscripts of the fifteenth and

a

b

Fig. 47   Early bronze processional crosses
(twelfth-thirteenth century?) in the monasteries of Debra Libanos, Eritrea (a and b)
and Abba Salama, Tigrai (c)

c

173

early sixteenth centuries are an unreliable guide. They do portray some simple processional crosses but the interesting designs which certainly ante-date those manuscripts do not figure in them at all. Probably the illuminators found them too complicated to draw and contented themselves with standard, simplified versions.

Those Abyssinian crosses which seem to be medieval mostly bear a family resemblance to each other. They have been referred to as 'Lalibela crosses' and, though many examples survive much further north, in Tigrai and Eritrea, they may well date from the times of the Agau kings who ruled from Lalibela for nearly three hundred years (*c.* 980–1270).

Plates 120–2   Usually made of copper or bronze, occasionally of iron, these crosses do not possess the square or diamond shape which later became so fashionable but are nevertheless full of originality. Their designers started elaborating simple cross-forms by

Fig. 47   breaking-up the cross itself (as seen in a and c on p. 173), by building up arched or angular frames round the central cross, or crosses (b); or by combining both these processes. The majority of the early crosses already have loops at their base, which may or may not be in one piece with the cross proper. Associated with the loops or the cross or both we find distinctive curved and pointed projections which appear to be the greatly stylized heads of doves: if so, they could be intended to symbolize the Holy Spirit, like the later and more obvious birds already mentioned in connection with priests' crosses.

Plates 118–19   Three other early processional crosses (all in the Museum of the Institute of Ethiopian Studies, Addis Ababa) are here repro-duced. The lower one is a rare and beautiful example which illustrates the transition from the medieval to the modern in cross design. It is built up round the simple cross-form which still stands out clearly as the core of the design, and tentative use is made of the diagonally-placed lesser crosses which, in some later designs, will completely fill the angles between the arms. The archaic engraved subjects in the central spaces provide supporting

Fig. 48 Late processional cross (seventeenth century) bearing engraved designs of western derivation: Crucifixion (top), Ecce Homo (left) and Resurrection (right) (from Scott)

175

evidence for the date of this cross which might be fifteenth or early sixteenth century.

Plates 123–6 Those varieties of the processional cross which today seem the most typical of Ethiopia were probably evolved in Gondar between 1600 and 1800. (A few have been dated on insecure grounds to the sixteenth or even the fifteenth century, but it is difficult to accept these datings.) As far as one can judge they are an indigenous creation owing little to any foreign influence, and they certainly are a notable contribution to the world repertory of decorative forms. The 'loops' which are invariably present in these crosses probably give some clue to their chronology. Plain loops, often attached in separate pieces, seem to belong to earlier crosses; more complex loops, integrated into the general design, to later ones, which are perhaps the finest.

Although they are so characteristically Abyssinian, one feature of these late crosses goes to prove that Western influences were at large at the time they were made, and this helps to establish their date more firmly. The influence in question is seen in the much simplified incised biblical subjects nearly always found when space for them is available. The iconography of most of Fig. 48 these subjects is unmistakably Western, and was unknown in Abyssinia before the seventeenth century (see p. 148). The cross on the previous page shows three examples.

The processional crosses provide a fitting conclusion to this survey of the Abyssinian arts. Whenever the *tabot* is carried in procession these splendid crosses will be in attendance, held aloft on tall poles. They must themselves be accompanied by the Fig. 9 gaudy canopies (or the umbrellas which are their modern substitute) which add still more colour to the brilliant and memorable scene. We may claim, furthermore, that the cross in this and other forms has received more varied and more original interpretations, and perhaps more devoted labour, in Ethiopia, than in any other Christian country.

Fig. 49   Small bronze processional cross (sixteenth century?) reconstructed from a fragment in the author's possession

Appendix A

The Ethiopic Syllabary

This Table, in which Semitic and other alphabets are compared, shows the very close dependence of the Ethiopic syllabary on the south-Arabian: it is thought to have been derived from a cursive rather than a monumental variety of the latter.

Each south-Arabian or Ethiopic character represents a syllable consisting of a consonant followed by a vowel, or a vowel alone. The nature of the vowel is not indicated either in the south-Arabian or the earliest Ethiopic script. However, a system of vocalization depending on modifications of the basic character was introduced by the Abyssinians in the fourth century A D.

Key: 1   Phonetic value
          2   Phoenician
          3   South-Arabian
          4   Ethiopic
          5   Hebrew
          6   Classical Greek
          7   Arabic

1	2	3	4	5	6	7
ʾ					A	
b					B	
g					Γ	z (ǧ)
d		(d)			Δ	d, ḏ (d)
h					E	
w					Y (?)	
z					Z	
ḥ		(ḫ)	(ḫ)		H	ḥ, ḫ (ḫ)
ṭ		(ẓ)			Θ	ṭ, ẓ (ẓ)
y					I	
k					K	
l					Λ	
m					M	
n					N	
s		(ś)			Ξ	
ʿ		(ǵ)			O	ʿ, ġ (ġ)
f (ph)					Π	
ṣ		(ḍ)			M	ṣ, ḍ (ḍ)
ḳ					Ϙ	
r					P	
š			(s)		Σ	
t		(t)			T	t, ṯ (t)
			T (p), (p)			

The Amharic Syllabary

The Amharic syllabary (see Table opposite) consists of all the original Ethiopic characters together with a number of additional ones. The first column gives the basic character or first form (as in previous Table); the second to seventh columns, the modified forms which express more definite vowel sounds following each consonant. The English transcription provided calls for the following explanations:

Consonants:

$k =$ explosive k
ñ   as in Spanish; French or Italian gn
kh $=$ ch in *loch*; German ch
zh $=$ s in *leisure*; French j
g   always hard
$t =$ explosive t
ch $=$ explosive ch
$p =$ explosive p

Vowels (Italian values are intended):

1st	form neutral as in French 'le'	
2nd	,,	long u
3rd	,,	long i
4th	,,	long a
5th	,,	long e
6th	,,	short i or no vowel
7th	,,	long o

1		2		3		4		5		6		7	
ሀ	hä	ሁ	hu	ሂ	hï	ሃ	hä	ሄ	hē	ህ	h, *or* hi	ሆ	ho
ለ	la	ሉ	lu	ሊ	lï	ላ	lä	ሎ	lō	ል	l, *or* li	ሎ	lo
ሐ	hä	ሑ	hu	ሒ	hï	ሓ	hä	ሔ	hē	ሕ	h, *or* hi	ሖ	ho
መ	ma	ሙ	mu	ሚ	mï	ማ	mä	ሜ	mē	ም	m, *or* mi	ሞ	mo
ሠ	sa	ሡ	su	ሢ	sï	ሣ	sä	ሤ	sē	ሥ	s, *or* si	ሦ	so
ረ	ra	ሩ	ru	ሪ	rï	ራ	rä	ሬ	rē	ር	r, *or* ri	ሮ	ro
ሰ	sa	ሱ	su	ሲ	sï	ሳ	sä	ሴ	sē	ስ	s, *or* si	ሶ	so
ሸ	sha	ሹ	shu	ሺ	shï	ሻ	shä	ሼ	shē	ሽ	sh, *or* shi	ሾ	sho
ቀ	*k*a	ቁ	*k*u	ቂ	*k*ï	ቃ	*k*ä	ቄ	*k*ē	ቅ	*k, or k*i	ቆ	*k*o
በ	ba	ቡ	bu	ቢ	bï	ባ	bä	ቤ	bē	ብ	b, *or* bi	ቦ	bo
ተ	ta	ቱ	tu	ቲ	tï	ታ	tä	ቴ	tē	ት	t, *or* ti	ቶ	to
ቸ	cha	ቹ	chu	ቺ	chï	ቻ	chä	ቼ	chē	ች	ch, *or* chi	ቾ	cho
ኀ	hä	ኁ	hu	ኂ	hï	ኃ	hä	ኄ	hē	ኅ	h, *or* hi	ኆ	ho
ነ	na	ኑ	nu	ኒ	nï	ና	nä	ኔ	nē	ን	n, *or* ni	ኖ	no
ኘ	ña	ኙ	ñu	ኚ	ñï	ኛ	ñä	ኜ	ñē	ኝ	ñ, *or* ñi	ኞ	ño
አ	ä	ኡ	u	ኢ	ï	ኣ	ä	ኤ	ē	እ	i	ኦ	o
ከ	ka	ኩ	ku	ኪ	kï	ካ	kä	ኬ	kē	ክ	k, *or* ki	ኮ	ko
ኸ	kha	ኹ	khu	ኺ	khï	ኻ	khä	ኼ	khē	ኽ	kh, *or* khi	ኾ	kho
ወ	wa	ዉ	wu	ዊ	wï	ዋ	wä	ዌ	wē	ው	w, *or* wi	ዎ	wo
ዐ	ä	ዑ	u	ዒ	ï	ዓ	ä	ዔ	ē	ዕ	i	ዖ	o
ዘ	za	ዙ	zu	ዚ	zï	ዛ	zä	ዜ	zē	ዝ	z, *or* zi	ዞ	zo
ዠ	zha	ዡ	zhu	ዢ	zhï	ዣ	zhä	ዤ	zhē	ዥ	zh, *or* zhi	ዦ	zho
የ	ya	ዩ	yu	ዪ	yï	ያ	yä	ዬ	yē	ይ	y, *or* yi	ዮ	yo
ደ	da	ዱ	du	ዲ	dï	ዳ	dä	ዴ	dē	ድ	d, *or* di	ዶ	do
ጀ	ja	ጁ	ju	ጂ	jï	ጃ	jä	ጄ	jē	ጅ	j, *or* ji	ጆ	jo
ገ	ga	ጉ	gu	ጊ	gï	ጋ	gä	ጌ	gē	ግ	g, *or* gi	ጎ	go
ጠ	*t*a	ጡ	tu	ጢ	*t*ï	ጣ	tä	ጤ	*t*ē	ጥ	*t, or t*i	ጦ	*t*o
ጨ	*ch*a	ጩ	*ch*u	ጪ	*ch*ï	ጫ	*ch*ä	ጬ	*ch*ē	ጭ	*ch, or ch*i	ጮ	*ch*o
ጰ	*p*a	ጱ	*p*u	ጲ	*p*ï	ጳ	*p*ä	ጴ	*p*ē	ጵ	*p, or p*i	ጶ	*p*o
ጸ	tsa	ጹ	tsu	ጺ	tsï	ጻ	tsä	ጼ	tsē	ጽ	ts, *or* tsi	ጾ	tso
ፀ	tsa	ፁ	tsu	ፂ	tsï	ፃ	tsä	ፄ	tsē	ፅ	ts, *or* tsi	ፆ	tso
ፈ	fa	ፉ	fu	ፊ	fï	ፋ	fä	ፌ	fē	ፍ	f, *or* fi	ፎ	fo
ፐ	pa	ፑ	pu	ፒ	pï	ፓ	pä	ፔ	pē	ፕ	p, *or* pi	ፖ	po

Appendix B

The Calendar, the Calculation of Easter, and the Dating of Manuscripts

THE CALENDAR

The calendars of the whole civilized world are based on the work of the old Egyptian astronomers who discovered, as early as three to four thousand years B C, that the solar or siderial year lasted slightly less than $365\frac{1}{4}$ days. However, it was left to the astronomers of the Alexandrian school, whose Hellenistic science enabled them to improve on early Egyptian astronomy, to incorporate this knowledge in a satisfactory calendar. It was they who devised the system of leap years whereby the calendar year could be kept in step with the natural year marked out by the seasons and the régime of the Nile.

If the Romans under Julius Caesar borrowed their reformed calendar from Alexandrian science, and bequeathed it to the western world, the Copts inherited this science as of right and built upon it themselves. In due course the Copts handed on this calendar, together with their method of computing the date of Easter, to their daughter Church in Ethiopia. The Coptic/Ethiopian year therefore has something in common with the western year, derived ultimately from the same sources. However, the years of their calendar are numbered from a different point of departure, have a different New Year's Day, are divided into different months, and have the extra day of Leap Year inserted at a different point.

The Coptic/Ethiopian calendar retains the old Egyptian system whereby the year was divided into twelve months, each of thirty days, plus five 'epagomenal' days at the end of the year; and the extra day required in Leap Year made a sixth day to that final, short, thirteenth 'month'. (N.B. See the slogan in current Ethiopian tourist literature: 'Thirteen months of sunshine'.)

Coptic/Ethiopian dates according to the 'Era of the Incarnation' (i.e. numbered from the year of Christ's birth) fall behind western dates by 7–8 years, and have done so since early Christian times. (Failing any indication of month and day, the rule is to add eight years to an Ethiopian date to obtain the equivalent year of the western calendar.) However, many dates used to be quoted according to a wholly different system—the 'Era of the World'. The starting point of this dating system was the conventional date—5,500 years before the birth of Christ—adopted for the Creation of the World; this put the beginning of the Christian Era in the year 5501.

During the third century the Alexandrian astronomers felt the need for a new starting point for the reckoning of dates which should take account of the moon's periodicity, so important for the calculation of Easter. They adopted the 19-year lunar cycle to which the Athenian scholar, Meton, had first drawn attention in the fifth century BC. (This simply meant that the phases of the moon recur on the same days of the month after an interval of nineteen years.) The year selected to inaugurate the new Era was 277 (Egyptian Era of the Incarnation) = AD 284, and the date taken for the New Year was equivalent to August 29 (Julian Calendar). These were no arbitrary choices. This date in this particular year was a New Moon and it reproduced the astronomical characteristics of the first day of Creation, since which event 5,776 years, or exactly 304 lunar cycles of 19 years, had elapsed.

This new Era, afterwards known as the Era of Diocletian (whose reign began in that year) or as the Era of the Martyrs, was widely used for dating purposes by both Copts and Abyssinians; the latter, however, preferred to begin numbering again after completion of the 'Grand Cycle' of 532 years when the phases of the moon were repeated, not only on the same dates, but on the same days of the week. The newly chosen New Year's Day (August 29, Julian; now September 11) became firmly established, no matter which method of reckoning years was thenceforth employed.

It must be mentioned, finally, that each Ethiopian year is dedicated to one of the four Evangelists according to the cycle: Matthew, Mark, Luke and John. The year of St Luke is Leap Year, the extra day being added to the short thirteenth month of the year (*Pagumen*). There is then an interval of less than three months before the beginning of the western Leap Year.

The following table shows the duration of the Ethiopian months in terms of the Western (Gregorian) calendar:

Maskaram	September 11 (12)	–	October 10 (11)
Tiqimt	October 11 (12)	–	November 9 (10)
Hidar	November 10 (11)	–	December 9 (11)
Tahisas	December 10 (11)	–	January 8 (9)
Tir	January 9 (10)	–	February 7 (8)
Yakatit	February 8 (9)	–	March 9
Magabit	March 10	–	April 8
Miaziya	April 9	–	May 8
Ginbot	May 9	–	June 7
Sané	June 8	–	July 7
Hamlé	July 8	–	August 6
Nahasé	August 7	–	September 5
Pagumen	September 6	–	September 10 (11)

Notes

A.   The dates in brackets apply only from the extra (intercalary) day added at the end of the Ethiopian Leap Year (Year of St Luke) until the extra day of the western Leap Year (February 29) which follows some $5\frac{1}{2}$ months later, and so restores the normal equivalence.

B.   It must be noted that before March 1, 1900, all the Gregorian dates given in the Table would have been one day earlier, before March 1, 1800, two days earlier, and before March 1, 1700, three days earlier. The reason for these alterations of equivalence in the years 1700, 1800 and 1900 is that the Ethiopians did not recognize the Gregorian reform whereby the intercalary day had to be suppressed in the last year of each century, which would otherwise be a Leap Year. However, according to the same reform, the year 2000 will *nevertheless* be a Leap Year, so the equivalence given in this Table will remain valid (unless the Ethiopians meanwhile revise their calendar) until February 28, AD 2100.

The Ethiopians are very much aware of the months of the year. But when speaking of events, past or future, they do not usually mention the days of the month, referring instead to certain festivals of the Church which recur monthly (on the same day of the month as the annual festival). The following are among those used as reference points of the months:

Day of the month	Festival
5	Gabra Manfas Qiddus (Abo)
7	Selassé = the Trinity
12	Mikael = the Archangel Michael
16	Kidané Meheret = The Covenant of Mercy
19	Gabriel = the Archangel Gabriel
21	Maryam = the Virgin Mary
23	Ghiorghis = St George
27	Medhané Alem = the Redeemer of the World
29	Yasus (Bala Wald) = the Nativity

Thus Maskaram Mikael means towards the middle of Maskaram; Hidar Bala Wald about the end of Hidar.

When times of day are mentioned or appointments made, it is important to remember that hours are reckoned from sunrise or sunset. Therefore, for example, the fourth hour of the day = 10 a.m.; the seventh hour of the night = 1 a.m.

THE CALCULATION OF EASTER

The Ethiopians recognize various characteristics of the year, i.e. *Tentyon* (day of the week of the first day of the year); Epact (age of the moon on the first day of the year), and *Matq'e* (in principle, the date of the first New Moon of the year). The latter must be used for determining the date of Easter and the complication is that, should the first New Moon of the year fall before Maskaram 15, *Matq'e* is postponed until the same date in the following month, which will not be New Moon at all. (This is to ensure that Easter should not fall too soon after the equinox.)

In arriving at the dates of the movable feasts, the Ethiopian Church, following the Coptic, does not use the western procedure of defining

Easter itself, and working backwards or forwards from that date. Instead, it works forwards from *matq'e* as follows:

To *matq'e* add:
Four months plus two to eight additional days (namely, as many as will make the day so reached a Monday). This gives the Fast of Nineveh, earliest of the ecclesiastical events that move with Easter.

To the date of Nineveh add:
14 days for the beginning of the Lenten Fast;
2 months and 9 days for Easter;
3 months and 28 days for Pentecost.

The dates on which Easter may fall range from Magabit 26 (April 4) until Miaziya 30 (May 8). While the western Easter can fall as early as March 22, a date closely following the Vernal Equinox, the Ethiopian Easter cannot fall less than a fortnight after the Equinox; nevertheless, in some years the Ethiopian and western dates coincide.

THE DATING OF MANUSCRIPTS

Scholars familiar with the calligraphy have established criteria by which earlier MSS. can be distinguished from the later. Though such changes in style are slight, dating on this basis is sometimes important as being the only available method. However, many MSS. are provided with a colophon at the end of the text in which the scribe defines the date on which his work was completed. One difficulty is that the colophon written in by a previous scribe (possibly centuries before) would sometimes be copied out word for word. However, if this source of error can be eliminated the colophon provides invaluable direct evidence of the manuscript's date.

Unfortunately the interpretation of the date given may still present difficulties, since the western system of dating from the birth of Christ is seldom used. As mentioned above, several different eras or astronomical cycles were used for dating purposes by the Copts and Ethiopians. These were:

(a) The Egyptian Era of the World, beginning on the date adopted for the Creation. (This was 5,500 years before the birth of Christ according to the Egyptian reckoning = B C 5492.) Dates called: 'Years of the World'.

(b) The Great Lunar Cycle or Grand Cycle of 532 years dating back to the Creation. (The first cycle was identical to (a); the beginning of the Christian Era fell in the 11th cycle.) Dates called: 'Years of Mercy'.

(c) The (Egyptian) Era of the Incarnation, dating from the birth of Christ. (Dates so expressed need to be corrected by the addition of 7 or 8 years to bring them in line with the western calendar.)

(d) The Era of Diocletian or Era of the Martyrs (beginning in the year 277 according to the Era of the Incarnation = A D 284).

(e) The Great Lunar Cycle or Grand Cycle of 532 years dating back to the same starting point as (d). (First cycle identical to (d); 2nd cycle began A D 817; 3rd cycle, A D 1349.) Dates called: 'Years of Mercy'.

As far as the dating of MSS. is concerned, system (d) was the one mainly used in Coptic Egypt but neglected in Ethiopia—an indication of the slight contact existing between these countries during the 'Golden Age' of Coptic literature (i.e. tenth to thirteenth centuries). The Ethiopians, on the contrary, favoured systems (a), (b) and (e).

During the fourteenth and fifteenth centuries both (b) and (e) were used, i.e. dates might be given according to either of two Great Lunar Cycles with distinct starting points, both called *amata meheret* (Year of Mercy) and giving results differing by 76 years. Happily the reign is usually given as well, so that the cycle actually in use can be identified. Two examples may be given:

(i) A famous illustrated MS. in the Bibliothèque Nationale, Paris, (d'Abbadie 105) is dated to the Year of Mercy 51, during the reign of King Ba'eda Maryam. This proves to be the 51st year of the 13th Great Lunar Cycle since the Creation = the year 1467 (Ethiopian reckoning) = A D 1475.

(ii) The Debra Maryam Gospels from which a number of illustrations are reproduced in this book is dated the 13th Year of Mercy in the reign of Seifa Ar'ada. This means the 13th year of the third Great Lunar Cycle in the Era of the Martyrs = 1353 (Ethiopian reckoning) = AD 1361.

From the sixteenth century onwards use is constantly made of the Year of the World. To take an example, subtracting 5,500 years, the date 7234 will indicate the year 1734 (Ethiopian reckoning) = AD 1742. Dates 'of Mercy' or 'of the Moon', i.e. according to one or other system of lunar cycles, are often added; so may be particulars of the reign, characteristics of the year (Evangelist, Epact, Matq'e, Tentyon) and the month and day on which the scribe completed his work. In addition the Year of the Incarnation may be quoted, and even, for good measure and greater confusion, the Year of the World according to the Byzantine reckoning.

Bibliography

The very restricted list given below includes only books and papers of which I have consciously made use in writing this book. For comprehensive bibliographies see the works of Budge, Doresse, Ullendorff, and others.

GENERAL AND CHAPTER I

BRYAN, M. A. *The Distribution of the Semitic and Cushitic Languages of Africa.* Oxford and New York, 1947.
BUXTON, D. R. *Travels in Ethiopia.* London, 1949. New York, 1967.
ETHIOPIAN STUDIES (papers read at the First International Conference of Ethiopian Studies). *Atti del Convegno Internazionale di Studi Etiopici.* Accademia Nazionale dei Lincei, Rome, 1960.
ETHIOPIAN STUDIES (papers read at the Second International Conference of Ethiopian Studies). *Journal of Semitic Studies,* Vol. IX, No. 1, Spring 1964.
GRAZIOSI, P. 'New Discoveries of Rock Paintings in Ethiopia' in *Antiquity,* Nos. 150/151, June and September 1964.
Guida dell'Africa Orientale Italiana. Milan, 1938.
LAST, G. C. 'The Geography of Ethiopia' in *Ethiopia Observer,* Vol. VI, No. 2, 1962.
PANKHURST, R. *An Introduction to the Economic History of Ethiopia from Early Times to 1800.* London and New York, 1961.
ULLENDORFF, E. *The Ethiopians.* Oxford, 1965. *Ethiopia and the Bible.* London and New York, 1968.

CHAPTER II

ANFRAY, F. 'Aspects de l'archéologie éthiopienne' in *Journal of African History,* Vol. IX, No. 3, 1968.
BECKINGHAM, C. F. and HUNTINGFORD, G. W. B. (editors). *The Prester John of the Indies* (the narrative of the Portuguese Embassy to Ethiopia in 1520, by Father Francisco Alvares). Hakluyt Society, London and Cambridge University Press, New York, 1961.

BUDGE, E. A. W. *A History of Ethiopia.* 2 Vols. London, 1928. *The Queen of Sheba and her only son Menyelek.* London and New York, 1932.
COULBEAUX, J.–B. *Histoire politique et religieuse de l'Abyssinie.* 3 Vols. Paris, 1929.
DORESSE, J. *L'empire du Prêtre-Jean.* 2 Vols. Paris, 1957.
DREWES, A. J. *Inscriptions de l'Ethiopie antique.* Leiden, 1962.
JONES, A. H. M. and MONROE, E. *A History of Abyssinia.* Oxford and New York, 1935. (New edition of 1955 entitled: *A History of Ethiopia.*)
KAMMERER, A. *Essai sur l'histoire antique d'Abyssinie.* Paris, 1926.
TRIMINGHAM, J. S. *Islam in Ethiopia.* London, 1952. New York, 1965.

CHAPTER III

BAETEMAN, J. *Dictionnaire amarigna-français.* Dire-Daoua, 1929.
BUXTON, D. R. 'The Shoan Plateau and its People' in *Geographical Journal,* Vol. CXIV, October–December 1949.
LEVINE, D. N. *Wax and Gold.* Chicago, 1965.
WALKER, C. H. *The Abyssinian at Home.* London and New York, 1933.

CHAPTER IV

BIDDER, I. *Lalibela.* Cologne, 1959.
BUXTON, D. R. 'The Christian Antiquities of Northern Ethiopia' in *Archaeologia,* Vol. XCII, 1947.
GERSTER, G. *Kirchen im Fels.* Stuttgart, 1968. English edition. *Churches in Rock.* London and New York, 1970.
LITTMANN, E., Krencker, D. and v. Lüpke, T. *Deutsche Aksum Expedition.* 5 Vols. Berlin, 1913. (Vol. 2, by Krencker, deals with early architecture).
MATTHEWS, D. H. and MORDINI, A. 'The monastery of Debra Damo, Ethiopia' in *Archaeologia,* Vol. XCVII, 1959.
MONTI DELLA CORTE, A. A. *Lalibela.* Rome, 1940.
MORDINI, A. La chiesa ipogea di Ucro (Amba Seneiti) nel Tigrai, in *Annali dell'Africa Italiana,* Anno 2, No. 2, 1939. Other important articles in *Rassegna di Studi Etiopici,* Vols. XII, 1953 and XV, 1959; *Annales d'Ethiopie,* Vol. IV, 1961; *L'Ethiopie d'Aujourd'hui,* Nos. 6–7, 1962; *Mélanges Eugène Tisserant,* Vol. III, 1964; etc.

SAUTER, R. Important articles in *Annales d'Ethiopie,* Vols. II, 1957 and V, 1963.

LECLANT, J., DE CONTENSON, H., ANFRAY, F. Individual and joint reports of excavations conducted on Axumite sites in *Annales d'Ethiope,* Vols. III, 1959; IV, 1961; V, 1963 and VI, 1965.

CHAPTER V

BUDGE, E. A. W. *The Miracles of the Blessed Virgin Mary and the Life of Hanna,* etc., (Lady Meux MSS 1–5). London, 1900.

CERULLI, E. *Storia della letteratura etiopica.* Rome, 1956.

CHAPTER VI

BUDGE, E. A. W. *The Lives of Maba Seyon and Gabra Krestos.* London, 1898. *The Miracles of the Blessed Virgin Mary.* London, 1900.

CERULLI, E. 'Il "Gesù percosso" nell'arte etiopica . . .' in *Rassegna di Studi Etiopici,* Vol. VI, 1947.

JÄGER, O. A. *Aethiopische Miniaturen.* Berlin, 1957.

LEROY, J. *Ethiopian Painting.* London and New York, 1967. (Italian and French editions published previously). 'L'évangéliaire éthiopien illustré du British Museum (Or. 510) et ses sources iconographiques' in *Annales d'Ethiopie,* Vol. IV, 1961. Other important articles in *Cahiers Archéologiques,* Vols. XI, 1960 and XII, 1962; etc.

MONNERET DE VILLARD, U. 'La Madonna di S. Maria Maggiore e l'illustrazione dei miracoli di Maria in Abissinia' in *Annali Lateranensi,* Vol. XI, 1947.

PLAYNE, B. *St. George for Ethiopia.* London and New York, 1954.

STAUDE, W. 'Etude sur la décoration picturale des églises Abba Antonios de Gondar et Dabra Sina de Gorgora' in *Annales d'Ethiopie,* Vol. III, 1959.

UNESCO WORLD ART SERIES. *Ethiopia, illuminated manuscripts* (with commentaries by J. Leroy, O. Jäger and S. Wright). Greenwich, Conn., 1961.

CHAPTER VII

BUDGE, E. A. W. *The Book of the Saints of the Ethiopian Church* (The Ethiopic Synaxarium). 4 Vols. Cambridge, 1928.

PICKEN, L. 'A note on Ethiopian Church Music' in *Acta Musicologica*, 1957.

POWNE, M. *Ethiopian Music*. Oxford and New York, 1968.

WELLESZ, E. J. 'Studien zur äthiopischen Kirchenmusik' in *Oriens Christianus*, N.S. 9–14, 1918–20. Contribution to *New Oxford History of Music*, II, 1954.

KORABIEWICZ, W.

PETRIDES, S. PIERRE

Neither of the above have yet published their work on Ethiopian crosses in permanent form, but they may be expected to do so at some future time.

APPENDIX B

CHAÎNE, M. *La Chronologie des temps chrétiens de l'Egypte et de l'Ethiopie*. Paris, 1925.

Periodicals concerned with all aspects of Ethiopian studies:

Annales d'Ethiopie. Addis Ababa and Paris, since 1955.
Ethiopia Observer. Addis Ababa and London, since 1956.
Journal of Ethiopian Studies. Addis Ababa, since 1963.
Rassegna di Studi Etiopici. Rome, since 1941.

Sources of Illustrations

I wish to express my best thanks to the following for kindly allowing me
to reproduce their photographs or drawings:—

Dr Georg Gerster for plates 48, 50, 56, 57 and 63, all taken from his
Kirchen im Fels (Churches in Rock); Dr Antonio Mordini for plate 78
and fig. 27; Miss Beatrice Playne for plates 80 and 81, which were
published in colour in the *Geographical Magazine*, February 1950, and
in *St. George for Ethiopia*, and for fig. 34 (a text figure from the last-
mentioned book after a photograph by myself); Frau Irmgard Bidder
for plate 55 and fig. 40 (from her *Lalibela*).

Mr D. H. Matthews, ARIBA, FSA, provided the photographs and
the drawing appearing in plates 51–53, 104 and fig. 8; the last two had
previously appeared in *Archaeologia*, vol. XCVII and the Society of
Antiquaries of London has agreed to my reproducing them here. Derek
Matthews also drew figs. 16 and 19 specially for this book, the former
from data supplied by me, the latter from his own intimate knowledge
of early Ethiopian building techniques.

Some of the text figures and plates were drawn from other publications.
as follows: figs. 4, 11–15, 17, 18, also plate 27, from the *Deutsche Aksum
Expedition;* fig. 6 from Bent's *Sacred City of the Ethiopians;* plates 91–2
from Budge's *Miracles of the Virgin Mary;* fig. 48 from *In the High Yemen*
by Hugh Scott, published by John Murray; figs. 23–4 (slightly modified)
from Monti della Corte's *Lalibela;* table 2 in Appendix A (slightly
abridged) from Alone-Stokes' *Short Manual of the Amharic Language*, by
permission of Macmillan & Co. Ltd.

Messrs Ernest Benn have permitted the re-use of five photographs
(plates 12, 13, 15, 28, 59) which appeared in my *Travels in Ethiopia*.
Other photographs of my own have been published before in *Archaeologia*, vol. XCII (plates 47, 49, 54, 58, 59, 97) and in the *Geographical
Journal*, vol. CXIV (plates 10, 11) and are now re-used with the approval
of the Society of Antiquaries and of the Royal Geographical Society;
the latter have also agreed to the inclusion of a re-drawn version of my
Debra Berhan map from the same paper (fig. 7).

About a hundred photographs taken by me (a few in 1949, most in 1969) are here published for the first time. For permission kindly given me to take and use some of these pictures I have to thank the following institutions in Addis Ababa: the National Museum for pre-Axumite museum pieces shown in plates 21–24, 26 (also fig. 3); the National Library for some pages of the Lake Hayq Gospels illustrated in plates 30, 76, 88 and figs. 31–2 (the Library's permission was given many years ago but the photographs had until now remained unused); the Institute of Ethiopian Studies, Haile Selassie I University, for crosses in plates 118–20 and the Madonna and Child, plate 79.

Mr Henry Littler let me photograph certain objects in his collection, two of which are shown in plates 94 and 117. Dr W. Korabiewicz was good enough to place several photographs of his own crosses at my disposal and these appear as plates 112–14. The only other photographs remaining unacknowledged are plates 4, 9 and 127, which are taken from anonymous Italian sources.

I am much indebted to the Keeper of Egyptian Antiquities at the British Museum and to the Keeper and Visitors of the Ashmolean Museum, Oxford, who let me examine and photograph some of the Coptic crosses in their collections. A selection of these were re-drawn and are now published in fig. 42 with the permission of the two museums. The portable altar from the Ashmolean, plate 103, is similarly published with their sanction.

Mr H. A. Shelley drew the four maps appearing as figs. 1, 2, 7 and 10, while Mr M. L. Rowe did numerous drawings for me, namely figs. 3, 5, 9, 20–1, 25–6, 28 (main subject), 30–3, 35, 37–9, 41–7 and 49. This volume owes much to their excellent work.

THE PLATES

15

17

19

20

21

22

23

24

25

26

27　　　28

እንዘ፡ሀሎኩ፡እኅ
ኅ፡ሕይወት፡ለብዕል
አኩ፡ኢሳሮን፡እንተ
ንደረት፡ደበሁ፡ተዱ
ኣ፡መንፈስ፡እጆ
ዕ፡አኩል፡ለዝክተ
ፀጋዎት፡ከጸ
ተፈ፡ለዘንጽር
ቃል፡ይትወህቤ፦
ከሙ፡በታላት፡ምን

ሱ፡ለተሻህፈ፡በአ
ኩ፡ጸሐፈ፡ለለአግርኽ
ሻሑፈ፡በእንተ፡ጽን
ዑ፡ምግባሩ፡ለለአክለ
ዐክ፡በኩሉ፡ጽኑዕ
ወቅዱክ፡ኣርፋንዮኩ
ዘሀገሩ፡ከሎዔናኽ
ዘሀገሩ፡ቲጸርኩ፡ጿ
ኩ፡ምስሉ፡ኢሳርዖ፡
ብዙኅ፡መዖሉ፡ሐየ
መስሊሁ፡ወዳ

ዙን፡ያስተርኢ፡ሥነኅ
ይከውኑ፡ተ፡ገጸ
ሩ፡ተደዮቶሙ፡ለፈሪ
ሳየን፡ወኢዮሐንኽ
በገዳፉ፡እንዘ፡ይሳው
ዑ፡ኢየሠምርሙ፡ወ
መንኒ፡በማክስ
ክዙን፡ስብእ፡በበለ
ዕ፡ወበስቲዩ፡ይዘንን
ፕዖ፡ወገሐቲታንን
ባኣ፡ውስተ፡ዘተዳዋ

30

ቲ፡ዘተሐጕለ፦
ፇኔ፡ምንት፡ትብሉ፡
ፈለእመቦ፡ዘቦቱ፡
ብእሲ፡ምእት፡አ
በጓዕ፡ወእውቃ
ገድፈ፡አሐዱ፡እ
ምውእቶሙ፦
አኮኑ፡ይነድግ
ትስዓ፡ወትስዓተ፡
ውስተ፡አድባር፡
ኢዱ፡ወየሐው
ረ፡የኅሥሥ፡ዘ
ተገድፈ፦
ወእምከውረከ
በ፡አማን፡እብለ
ከሙ፡ከሙ፡ይት

በቅድመ፡አቡየ፦
ዘበሰማያት፡ከመ
ይትሐጐል፡አሐ
ዱ፡እምእሉ፡ንኡ
ሣን፦
የጽዕ፡ወእመሪ፡አበከ
ፈ፡ለከ፡እኁከ፡ሐር
ወገሥጾ፡በባሕ
ቲትክሙ፡አንተ
ውእቱ፡ወለእመ
ክ፡ሰምዐከ፡ነሀ
ተረባሕከ፡ለእኁከ
የጽዕ፡ወለእመሰ፡ኢ
ሰምዐከ፡ንሣእ
ምስሌከ፡በደገ
ም፡አሐደ፡ወከ

31   32

33

34

35

36

37

38

39

40

41

42

43

44

45

46

49

50

56

57

58

62

64

63

65

68

69

70

71

72

73

74

75

76

77

78

79

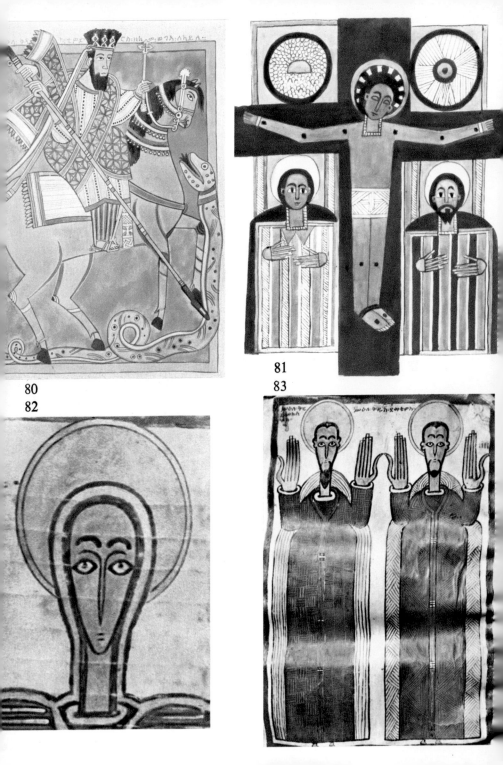

80

82

81

83

84

85

86

87

88

89

90

91

92

94

93

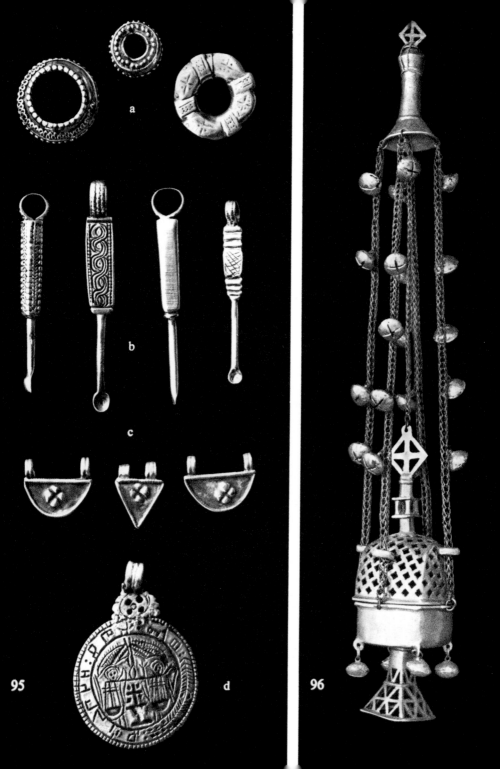

95

a

b

c

d

96

97

98

99

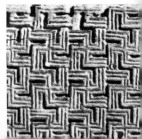

100

101

102

103

104

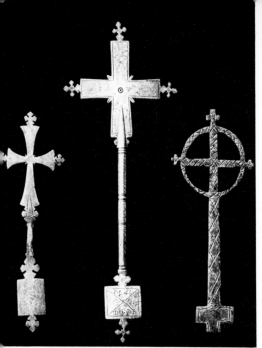

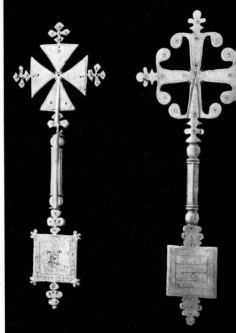

106 - 108

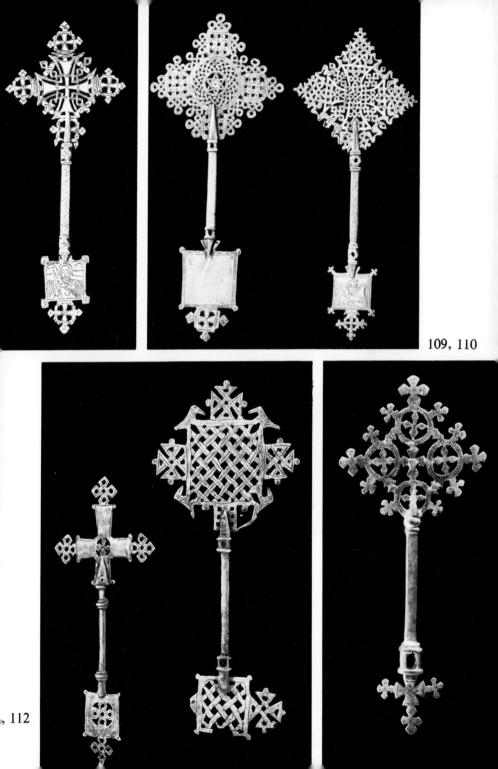

109, 110

, 112

113

114

115

16

17

118

119

120

121

122

123

124

125

126

127

128

Notes on the Plates

1–3 Amharas of Shoa. The small boy's tufted hairstyle is characteristic.

4 Woman of Tigrai with braided hair, in contrast to the Shoan style (3).

5 Village elders, district of Seraé, Eritrea.

6 Abbot of a monastery in Tembien, Western Tigrai, at work on a manuscript. He wears the usual monk's cap.

7 Market women at Atsbi, eastern highlands of Tigrai.

8 Tigrean priest wearing turban, and carrying his cross and fly-whisk.

9 Ethiopian meal (Eritrea). The family eats off a raphia *masob* which just takes the round sheets of local bread *(injera)*. This, together with a peppery sauce *(wat)* forms the basis of Ethiopian food.

10 The Shoan plateau near Debra Berhan—short grass country at about 3,000 m. (10,000 feet). The festival of Timqet is being celebrated.

11 One of the deep gorges (of the Blue Nile system) which carve up the high plateau west of Debra Berhan in Shoa. The gorge here is nearly 600 m. (2,000 feet) deep and populated 'shelves' are seen at two levels.

12 Liturgical dance in progress on St Michael's annual festival. The *dabtaras,* holding their prayer-sticks, are in two rows facing each other; drummers are seen to left and right.

13 Typical rectangular country church in Tigrai.

14 Small round country church of Shoa, near Debra Berhan. It is dedicated to Abuna Gabra Manfas Qiddus (Abo) whose festival is being celebrated.

Domestic architecture of northern Ethiopia. (15–18)

15 Two-storeyed round houses, and compound wall with gatehouse, at Sokota in Waag, Wallo province.

16 Flat-roofed, rectangular habitations in dry-stone masonry, Tigrai province.

17–18 Columned front and interior of monastic buildings at Debra Merkurios, Seraé district. Although these belong to a monastery, they resemble ordinary dwellings in this part of Eritrea.

19–20 Temple of Yeha, *c.* fifth century B C. Interior view and 'stepped' courses at the foot of the outer wall. (cf. text figure 11)

Pre-Axumite objects now in the National Museum, Addis Ababa: mostly fifth to fourth century B C. (21–24)

21–22 Ibexes in relief from the throne of Haoulti (each panel *c.* 6 cm. square) and a black stone bull from Melazo (8.5 cm. long). Both the ibex and the bull were attributes of the god Almaqah, whose cult was introduced from Southern Arabia.

23 Statue of a female figure with elaborate counter-poised necklace from Haoulti. Height 80 cm.

24 Rectangular incense-burner or fire-altar with architectural decoration and the crescent-and-disk symbol of Almaqah. The foot restored. Height 40 cm. Round ones are also known.

South Arabian and Ethiopic lettering. (25–30)

25 Part of a monumental inscription in a south Arabian dialect at Yeha. Height of each block *c.* 13 cm. Fifth century B C?

26 Inscribed limestone altar with stepped base dedicated to Almaqah. Height 44 cm. The top is scooped out to form a shallow depression, 15 × 11.5 cm. The south-Arabian inscription is 'boustrophedon', i.e. the lines run alternately right to left and left to right.

27 Ethiopic inscription of King Ezana, from *Deutsche Aksum Expedition*

(inscription No. 10), retouched. Fourth century A D. The syllabary is already vocalized.

28 Inscribed grave stone at Ham, Eritrea. Eighth century A D? It is among the latest known Ethiopic inscriptions.

Pages from manuscripts written on parchment. (29–30)

29 Decorative chapter heading from a large copy of the *Gadla Abau* (Acts of the Fathers) formerly in Addis Ababa. Late fourteenth or early fifteenth century. The whole page measures 58×40 cm.; the three-columned text is here reduced by half.

30 Part of a two-columned page from the Lake Hayq Gospels now in the National Library, Addis Ababa. First half of the fourteenth century. Page height 30 cm. The script is here reproduced about actual size.

Axumite remains, third to fourth centuries A D. (31–46)

–32 Stepped and 'indented' podia of secular buildings (palaces?) at Adi Kilté near Axum and at Matara near Senafé, Eritrea ('Tertre A'). These are typical Axumite foundations.

–34 Monumental main stairway of the palace at Adi Kilté, Axum, and a double-flighted back stair of the same building.

35 Axumite column and stepped capital (not belonging together) in the public garden, Axum.

–37 Heads of columns with stepped capitals carved from the same block lying on the sites of Adulis (Red Sea coast) and Tokonda (high plateau of Eritrea). They identify both these very different sites as Axumite.

–39 Axumite bases of stepped form now in the public garden at Axum. In 38 each 'step' has a segmental protrusion in the centre; this complex base was intended for a wooden column. 39 was for a fluted octagonal column whose base is in position.

The Axum monoliths with their architectural decoration. (40–44)

40 Detail from side of collapsed giant monolith of thirteen storeys.

41 Base of the monolith still standing, showing simulated door with latch.

42 The erect, ten-storeyed monolith standing 21 m. (70 feet) high.

43 Broken apex of a relatively small monolith in the precincts of St Mary of Zion, Axum.

44 Carved windows from the topmost storeys of the giant monolith showing a type of ornamental window-infilling based on miniature arches. (cf. text figure 16)

45–46 Typical votive thrones at Axum showing slots for the upright slabs which have all disappeared. Cf. text figure 13.

Medieval built-up churches (three of them standing in caves) showing continued use of Axumite building techniques. (47–55)

47 Yemrahana Kristos, Lasta district.

48 Debra Selam near Atsbi, eastern Tigrai.

49 Debra Libanos near Ham, Eritrea. Now destroyed.

50 Mekena Medhane Alem, Lasta.

51 Debra Damo: the sanctuary seen through the sanctuary arch, with frieze and dome.

52 Debra Damo: detail of sanctuary arch and frieze.

53 Debra Damo: nave with monolithic columns carrying lintels, and frieze.

54 Yemrahana Kristos: windows of the east end with carved wooden infillings.

55 Yemrahana Kristos: roof and upper nave walls with frieze.

Rock-hewn churches showing imitation of timber forms from built up structures. (56–65)

56 Aerial view of the monolithic church of St George, Lalibela. It is carved from a single block of rock left standing in an excavated pit. Thirteenth to fourteenth century?

57 St Mary, Lalibela; view from the south aisle north-eastwards across the

nave, showing double capitals, elaborately carved arches (cf. plate 97) and frieze. This is the most lavishly carved of all rock-hewn interiors. Twelfth to thirteenth century?

58 South side of Emmanuel, Lalibela. It is a careful copy of Axumite wall-structure.

59 South-west corner of the monolithic church of Ghenetta Maryam, Lasta, with its massive external colonnade. Fourteenth century?

Interiors of three 'cruciform' rock-hewn churches in the province of Tigrai. Twelfth century? (60–62)

60 Cherqos Wuqro: diagonal view from south aisle across western arm of cross (frieze visible upper right) into north arm of cross with window.

61 Abreha Atsbeha: view from north arm of the cross through the middle bay (with imitated crossed beams) into the south arm, with frieze and elaborately decorated 'barrel vault'.

62 Amba Mikael, Tigrai. Diagonal view across south arm showing Axumite pillars, capitals, lintels and frieze.

63 Emmanuel, Lalibela. East end of nave with frieze running above arches and sanctuary dome visible through paired windows. Twelfth to thirteenth century?

64 St George, Lalibela. Dome over sanctuary and ogee windows. Four-teenth century?

65 Abba Yohanni, Tembien district of Tigrai. Eastward view in north aisle showing a domed bay and late type of frieze. Fifteenth century?

66 Wuqro Maryam in Derà, north of Atsbi in the eastern highlands of Tigrai. Only the top storey of this remarkable structure is the church proper, which is extended internally by excavation. The architecture is related to that of built-up village churches in Tigrai. (cf. plate 13)

67 Enda Abuna Yonas in Kohain, Eritrea—a singular monastic church approached by a rock-climb from the far side.

Small paintings, mostly from manuscripts. (68–83)

68–75 Illustrations from a gospel-book found by the author in January 1949 at the monastery of Debra Maryam in Kohain, Eritrea. It has since been disastrously damaged. The Passion sequence includes a Transfiguration (68); Arrest of Christ and Peter's Denial (69); Crucifixion (70); Entombment (71); Resurrection (72); Ascension (73). The two Evangelists whose portraits form frontispieces to their Gospels are a standing St Mark (74) and a seated St Luke (75).

76 Page from the Eusebian canons preceding the text of the Lake Hayq Gospels, now in Addis Ababa. First half of the fourteenth century.

77 'Fountain of Life' from the end of the canon tables, Gospels of Yehyeh Ghiorghis. Middle of the fifteenth century.

78–79 Abyssinian versions of the Madonna and Child, who are invariably protected by the Archangels Michael and Gabriel with raised swords. 78 is from a manuscript of the fifteenth century at Gunda Gunde, showing very pronounced Ethiopian stylization, 79 from a later diptych, now in the Institute of Ethiopian Studies, Addis Ababa. The transfer of the Child from the right to the left arm, and the twig held by both figures, are signs of western influence.

80 An equestrian saint, St Theodore the General, spears the man-eating serpent which figures in his legend. The guiding hand of the Almighty grasps the spear above his own. From a *Lives of the Saints* at Debra Maryam in Kohain, Eritrea. Fifteenth century. This and plate 81 copied by Beatrice Playne in the 1940s.

81 Highly stylized Crucifixion from a folded parchment strip formerly at Lalibela, now lost. Seventeenth century?

82–83 Illustrations from the *Acts of the Fathers*, formerly in Addis Ababa (cf. plate 29). Probably early fifteenth century. 82 shows a head of St Eupraxia (Euphrasia) and 83 the saintly brothers Maximus and Dumatheus, with hands upheld in the early Christian attitude of prayer.

Painted rock-hewn walls and dome of the church of Yadibba Maryam in Daunt, Wallo province. The photographs were taken in 1949 when this sanctuary was disused and therefore accessible (84–85).

84 Domed ceiling of sanctuary of St George.

85 The approach to the sanctuary, showing David and Solomon (upper left).

86 Traditional ceiling (with winged cherubs' heads of western inspiration) in the church of Debra Merkurios, Seraé, Eritrea, reconstructed about 1947.

87 Modern diptych with paintings on cloth of the two most popular Ethiopian saints. Left, Abuna Gabra Manfas Qiddus (Abo) always shown with attendant animals; Satan is attacking him in the form of a bird and as a demon (whose hands are smitten off by an angel). Right, Abuna Tekla Haymanot, always represented with three pairs of wings. He stood in a cell for many years until his right leg withered and dropped off.

–90 The Flight into Egypt in Ethiopian manuscript illustrations, showing the very late manifestation of local colour. The Virgin's sister or maid-servant Salome is always shown. 88 is from the Hayq Gospels (Addis Ababa) fourteenth century. Joseph, guided by an angel, carries the Child Jesus on his shoulders (cf. a mosaic in the Capella Palatina, Palermo, Sicily). 89 is an eighteenth-century manuscript illustration from Gondar. Salome's food-basket and Joseph's prayer-stick are Abyssinian. 90 shows the same subject from Mahedere Maryam, district of Debra Tabor, and is also eighteenth century. Local influence has at length prevailed against traditional iconography.

Illustrations from a copy of the *Miracles of the Virgin Mary*, formerly in the possession of Lady Meux and edited by Budge. Seventeenth century. (91–92)

91 A painter is shown working in a church on a scaffolding (his subjects being Paradise and Hell). He is thrown down by demons (lower left) but the Virgin Mary stretches out her hand from her picture and saves him.

92 Three Arabs are cast into the water when their boat is wrecked. The two who cried to the Virgin Mary reach a rock and are saved, but the third man is swallowed by a crocodile. One of those saved vows a camel and a load of dates to the Virgin's shrine (lower right) and afterwards redeems his vow (above).

93 Silver *birelé*, 14 cm. high. It is modelled on the glass vessels used for drinking *tej*, the Abyssinian mead.

94 Ornamental cup in silver alloy, 9 cm. high. Its shape resembles that of ordinary country drinking vessels.

95 The silver rings (a) ear-picks (b) and *pendeloques* (c) are strung on women's necklaces. 95(d) is an old Abyssinian personal seal (3.5 cm. in diameter) which has been adapted as a pendant.

96 Bronze censer, modern but traditional.

Church woodwork. (97–104)

97–98 Segments of arches and loose panels (probably derived from a *manbar* or frieze). Saved from a demolished church at Aramo, Eritrea, and now in the Asmara museum. (cf. Plate 52)

99 Geometrical panels forming part of an 'altar' *(manbara tabot)* at Debra Selam near Atsbi, Tigrai.

100–101 Two examples of wooden *tabots*—the consecrated slabs which are the essential element of a church. Those illustrated measure $9\frac{1}{2} \times 11 \times 4$ cm. (100) and *c.* 22 cm. square (101).

102–103 Portable altars carved from one piece of wood. They have a cavity for small *tabots* closed by a hinged door (missing in 103). 102 from Maryam Aba's in Atsbi-Derà. Height *c.* 50 cm. 103 now in the Ashmolean Museum, Oxford. Height 35 cm.; cavity 9×7 cm. $\times 13$ cm. deep.

104 Ceiling panels in the main church at Debra Damo, Tigrai, possibly as early as the eighth century. Although some of the carved animals (e.g. elephant and ibex) might be local, all these subjects (including some fabulous creatures) are probably of Asian derivation. The cow suckling her calf (middle panel, second row) is closely paralleled in Mesopotamian cylinder seals. The geometrical panels have probably been inserted later.

Crosses in metal and wood. (105–126)

105 Silver pectoral crosses, slightly reduced.

106–112 Metal priests' crosses, varying in length between 17 and 30 cm. 106–8 are iron, 109–10 silver, 111–12 brass. The softer metals of the last two categories allow of complicated openwork designs. Note stylized birds in 110 (right) and 111 (right).

16 Wooden priests' crosses, their lengths varying between 24 and 47 cm.

17 Miniature double diptych with pierced flange for suspension, measuring 7.5×6.5 cm. (cf. text figure 33)

Processional crosses of intermediate age (*c.* fifteenth century?) in the museum of the Institute of Ethiopian Studies, University of Addis Ababa. (118–119)

18 Left, iron cross from Debra Tabor. Right, bronze (?) cross from Lasta district, about 18 cm. high—unusually small for a processional cross.

19 Possibly a reliquary cross. Gilded bronze, with archaic engravings of Christ, the Apostles, and Archangels.

22 'Lalibela crosses' in copper or bronze, twelfth to thirteenth century (?) A specimen (35 cm. high) in the Institute of Ethiopian Studies, Addis Ababa (120), one at Lalibela (121), and one held by the abbot of Abba Yohanni in Tembien (122).

26 Processional crosses in various metals, seventeenth century or later. The example in 124 measures 38 cm.; those in 125–6 (at Debra Maryam in Kohain) are much larger.

27 Eritrean ecclesiastic with crown and processional cross.

28 Back of a small brass lectern from Eritrea, probably eighteenth century. A third cross is missing from the upper lunette. The middle figure is Ewostatewos (Eustathius), indicating that the lectern was used by monks of his order. The flanking figures, who both adopt the early Christian praying attitude, are the Ethiopian saints Tekla Haymanot and Gabra Manfas Qiddus.

Index